*From a Shore Beyond Water: Selected Poems*
Copyright © 2023 Daniel Abdal-Hayy Moore
All rights reserved.

For quotes any longer than those for critical articles and reviews, contact:
The Ecstatic Exchange,
6470 Morris Park Road, Philadelphia, PA 19151-2403
email: abdalhayy@danielmoorepoetry.com

**FIRST EDITION**
ISBN: 979-8-9877984-0-9
Published by The Ecstatic Exchange,
6470 Morris Park Road, Philadelphia, PA 19151-2403

Also available from The Ecstatic Exchange:
*Knocking from Inside*, poems by Tiel Aisha Ansari

Cover art by Salihah Moore, using elements from many of
Daniel Abdal-Hayy Moore's collages from his book covers.

Inside frontispiece (letter *waw*s embracing) by Soraya Syed.

Typesetting and design by Mukhtar Sanders, Inspiral Design.

# FROM A SHORE BEYOND WATER

SELECTED POEMS

*of*

Daniel Abdal-Hayy Moore

THE ECSTATIC EXCHANGE

2023

Philadelphia

DANIEL ABDAL-HAYY MOORE
*1940–2016*

# PRAISE FOR DANIEL ABDAL-HAYY MOORE'S WORK

This is an enthusiastic general recommendation and appreciation of The Floating Lotus Magic Opera Company, whose director is Daniel Moore. ...It is rather impossible to describe or characterize these productions, but it is enough to say that there has never been anything like it in the theater or in the opera or, for that matter, in the world... [It is] a unique and beautiful ceremonial genre, a ritual drama not seen or heard before.

LAWRENCE FERLINGHETTI,
*Poet, Founder of City Lights Books, writing in 1969*

The intelligence of Daniel Moore's poems is like Frank O'Hara's: there are no boundaries or limits to possible subject matter. Imagination runs rampant and it glides. Reading them is like standing in a cool snow field on a sunny day. It's a blanket of glory and a sheer act of beauty... Moore is unique in the variance and perfection of his prosody. Each poem is a new melody. Like the metaphysical poets, Vaughn, Herbert, Crashaw, the shape of the poem is strong, no matter how lovely; it is fused with depth. This is the real thing!

MICHAEL MCCLURE, *Beat Poet, Critic*

[From a Shore Beyond Water] gave me a sense of recognition. A reaffirmation of a reality. THE reality. *La ilaha ill'Allah.* The peculiar and plain. An enthusiastic loving reminder of the always-expanding nature of beauty and truth. And the source of all beauty and truth.

YASIIN BEY, *Artist*

One of those truly inspired and illuminated souls, Abdal-Hayy Moore invites us to awaken to the awe and ecstasy of existence itself. Through poetic flashes of light, he calls us to see the world for what it is – a miraculous symphony of meaning unfolding before our eyes and within our very beings.

BARAKA BLUE, *Poet, Musician, Rumi Center for Spirituality & The Arts*

The Master, Ibn ʿArabi, says that when all we have is the horizontal slant on reality, we can only see Jalal (the Majestic), which means God is hidden… On the horizontal level, complex scientific and humanities knowledge "tie up the soul in knots," which he calls "knots of the soul." Daniel Abdal-Hayy Moore is blessed with the vertical connection, which, the Master says, cuts these Gordian knots of the soul. Then we are able to see Jamal (the Beautiful) in Jalal, and all creation speaks.

DR. UMAR FARUQ ABD-ALLAH WYMANN-LANDGRAF,
*Scholar, The Oasis Initiative, Chicago*

Daniel Abdal-Hayy Moore is really at the vanguard of a cultural movement within our ranks, of creating an indigenous Muslim art form that reflects the best of our culture. He's an American poet who was writing poetry in the 60s in San Francisco and recognized by his peers as being a poet of merit, and then became a Muslim and developed his own art form within Islam. This is what we need, an indigenous Islam that emerges from this country, rooted in this soil.

SHAYKH HAMZA YUSUF, *Zaytuna Institute*

From beekeepers in the mountains to exotic birds in the desert, Daniel Moore always travels to the essential question of who we are, why we are here, and where we are going.

SHEMS FRIEDLANDER, *Filmmaker, Teacher, Author,
Former Emeritus Professor of Practise at the American University in Cairo*

Daniel Abdal-Hayy Moore has combined the strong and spontaneous strain of American free verse that flows up through Whitman, Williams, and Ginsberg with the deep well of his Islamic devotion… He's like an old wisdom tradition come up off the streets.

COLEMAN BARKS, *Poet, Versions of Rumi*

I don't think anyone's accomplished quite this kind of thing since Mr. Walt.

MICHAEL WOLFE, *Poet*

Daniel Moore is that rarity among his contemporaries – a surrealist of the sacred
– whose poems are shimmering cornucopias of xylophones, gazelles, minarets and
herons, spilling forth their abundance, the seen and the Unseen, suffused with
spiritual awe and love of God. In these pages we are in the presence of a visionary
servant of the divine, a poet of torrential imagination, in whose hands we are all
whooshed into the world of spirit.

CAROLYN FORSCHÉ,
*Poet, Editor, Translator, Professor, Human Rights Advocate*

Moore was a legend among poets and the hip cognoscenti of California in the
1960s, so it's a great pleasure to see just how brightly this flame still burns. The eye
and ear have retained every ounce of sharpness. Can a deeply spiritual poet have
this much humor? Imagine Mayakovsky, McClure and Frank O'Hara all wrapped
into one.

RON SILLIMAN, *Poet, Critic*

Moore is disturbing. If we want him to be a Muslim poet, he leads us through the
winding alleyways and open deserts of Islam, letting us imbibe its perfumes – but
then returns and takes us into the American Beat Ferlinghetti underground. Or if
we want to go with him – on the road – with a howl – he'll show us city lights, but
then he whirls and sends us, heads facing down, bodies prostrate on carpets, spirits
flying, toward Mecca and beyond… To read Moore is to journey.

DR. ALAN 'ABDAL-HAQQ GODLAS,
*Associate Professor, Dept. of Religion, University of Georgia*

I celebrate Daniel Moore's unique and constant creative work over the decades.
"Visionary" means truly seeing truth unveiled, seeing within and without the
inescapable unity of all facets and aspects of the Divine – and sometimes being able
to frame the unsayable in language. It is this poetry that he has been mastering over
the years – no mean feat; in fact, it is an extraordinary enterprise of inestimable
value and inspiration.

DAVID MELTZER, *Beat Poet, Musician*

Moore is an unacknowledged giant, master craftsman of the spiritual poem of our age, triple heir to Emerson and the Sufi poets and the Zen teachers, a bearded beatnik *murid* Muslim poet taking us with him on the path, thawing our hearts in a thoroughly American landscape.



Abdal-Hayy lives the poetic life. He is the real thing. He has been there. He has seen it, written of it, and come to tell us, in his own voice, all about it. If you want to know what "it" is, ask him and he will tell you, with cosmic music, with wit, with the intensity of a well-banked fire that warms but never burns.



A sweet current of sacred humor runs through these poems [which] should be especially appreciated by those of us trying to follow a traditional way at this point in time and space, "wearing both coarse cloth and tailored suits" for our various meetings with God's Names of Beauty and Rigor. My profound thanks to Daniel Abdal-Hayy Moore for this generous gift.



I've always thought that poet Daniel Abdal-Hayy Moore is a kind of Lewis Carroll in reverse – forsaking our now-established Looking Glass World (instead of falling into or for it) in favor of a post-surrealist, often comedic God-fixated world. Daniel is a Sufi, but one who owes as much to André Breton and Garcia Lorca as he does Rumi and Kabir.



One cannot know poetry, especially not spiritual poetry, until one tastes the work of Moore firsthand.

# DEDICATED TO

Shaykh Muhammad Ibn al-Habib ﷺ
and
Sufi Shaikh Muhammad Raheem Bawa Muhaiyaddeen رَحَهُ اللّٰه
and all *shuyukh* of instruction and *ma'arifa*
*Alhamdulillah*

✳

*The earth is not bereft
of Light*

# CONTENTS

# IN MEMORIAM

There is so much I want to say about my dad. There are things not everyone knew about him. For example, how animals loved him. He never killed spiders, but instead carefully escorted them outside in cups. Or that time a hornet was in the house, and after Dad performed an improv wasp-inspired dance, the hornet flew right into his cup – zzzzzzp! How he rescued that injured possum from being roadkill – he named her Blossom the Possum.

People probably didn't know that he picked up trash every day during his morning walk in the neighborhood park, that he was the best at handmade cards, that he was always poignant and hilarious. Everyone who knew him can tell you about his charismatic wit and sense of humor. He was a wonderful storyteller. He had so many adventures from his time with the Beat poets, from living in Mexico, directing ritual theater in Berkeley in the 60s, being with Sufi sheikhs in Morocco, Nigeria, and beyond.

His spirit was kind and exuberant. He talked to everyone – in the grocery line, at the airport, and especially if you were a Muslim taxi driver. He had a beautiful singing voice and could sit down at a piano and play the most incredible song despite no training in music. He had a wealth of knowledge from music, literature, films, poetry (of course), crossword trivia; he knew all the Jeopardy answers. He had thousands of books and knew where every single one was. He was very smart, a master of words, and everyone thought he would be famous, but instead he gave up writing for ten years to devote himself to Islam.

He was a mystic, twinkle-eyed man with both feet firmly on the ground, yet he dressed up like the tooth fairy when we lost our baby teeth. He did shadow plays for us, we had skit nights, and we were always drawing each other on napkins at restaurants. He never left home without a pen and often wrote poetry in the middle of the night, awakened by strange dreams. He had a mermaid toothbrush. He collected an assortment of knick-knack treasures found at yard sales, he played harmonica and zither, he always had a pen and a handkerchief in his pocket. Fluent in Spanish and French, he loved talking in different languages and worked on translations. He was a visionary 60s icon turned devotee, and he stuck with it, reciting the *shahadah* with his last breath. We miss him...but when I return to his poetry, I find his sweet voice again and all the brilliant wisdom of his ecstatic exchange still here, in this world, with us.

SALIHAH MOORE
*Boulder, Colorado*
*April 2018*

# INTRODUCTION

Abdal-Hayy's art was born out of a particular fraternity of poets. In a time when the Freedom Movement, the impact of the Vietnam War and Flower Power converged in American culture, these poets – like Alan Ginsberg, Lawrence Ferlinghetti, Michael McClure, Diane Di Prima, Amiri Baraka and Sonia Sanchez – were rewriting the American canon. Abdal-Hayy felt the call of peace, love, and beauty, but there was something that Haight Ashbury couldn't fill. It was this emptiness that led him to the path of Allah and the Messenger.

Abdal-Hayy's work always feels timely, urgent, and relevant. It is poetry that connects us to the universal, to the timeless, by precisely speaking to us in our time and to our condition. The people around Abdal-Hayy were incredibly diverse. His poetry was like the home that Malika and he created – a place where a lot of different people gathered, confessed, and spoke their hearts. And while Abdal-Hayy maybe wasn't engaged in a particular type of "activism," I think he looked upon those who did with not just respect, but also awe and support, constantly sending them *du'as* (prayers) and love, honoring and elevating them. His poems stood with them like pillars of strength to lean on.

Some of Abdal-Hayy's poetry deals with pain and the deep suffering that comes with being human. An example of this is "Train Wreck in Reverse," one of the first of Abdal-Hayy's poems I was introduced to. It captured my ear and imagination. It is a difficult poem, one that takes the reader back into the small, prosaic moments before a train crash. It is a poem that gives you chills, because it makes you achingly aware of how an instant can change everything. It is a poem which warns against complacency. Through the horror of tragedy, Abdal-Hayy leaves us with the unshakeable truth that every moment is God-given and precious. Abdal-Hayy's poetry is all about those little moments we tend to forget – or ignore. He finds the beauty in those small spaces.

Some of those small spaces exist in us. The dark, fragmented places which cloud our *fitra* (innate spiritual nature) and produce anxiety and unease.

Abdal-Hayy is unafraid of those places. He treads thoughtfully, taking care not to break something that is already weakened or harm something that needs to heal. And I think that when people who are engaged in the work of world-changing and world-building, of challenging things like white supremacy, anti-Black racism, misogyny, sexism, economic marginalization, or state violence read Abdal-Hayy's poetry, they find it manna for their souls. To read Abdal-Hayy is to be nourished. It is at once to be held – and to be blown wide open.

Muslimness has been woven into the fabric of this place that we call America since non-Indigenous people began to arrive on its shores. Some Muslims came to conquer, subdue, and subjugate. Others came subjugated, ripped from their homes, their humanity denied. It was those who came in chains who found ways to keep their culture, faith, and their memories alive. The sound of the field hollers, gospel, blues, and jazz all carry the DNA of Muslim cultures, from Africa most significantly, and elsewhere. Into this "American" culture, the connection to God and the Prophet, the prayers, the rituals, the metaphysics, the worldviews, and the stories are inseparably woven in. Abdal-Hayy's work grows out of who he was, and when Muslimness became a part of him, he wove that into his work, too. The tapestry of his art became richer, its colors more vibrant, its designs more mesmerizing.

This is a gift that Allah gives to some people who have been blessed with the right receptors. We as communities need to create space for the people with receptors to pick up Divine signals – artists, poets, filmmakers, musicians, writers. They give their gift to us through their art. Of course, those voices are going to be disruptive. Abdal-Hayy's poetry is challenging. It forces us to look at ourselves. He speaks about the human, about love and sensuality, about conflict and death. That's why his poetry is so universal. His work should encourage other artists, who come from the same tradition as him, to be bold and unapologetic.

The message his poetry gives to cultural producers is: Do your art. Write your poetry, make your music, film your films, record your podcasts, draw your paintings, tag your wall, spit 16 bars, speak the words. Put it out there, and know that it's coming from this soul engine, connected to the Divine, who we believe is animating us, who is sustaining us, who is closer to us than ourselves.

Abdal-Hayy's words remind me of the words of Baba Bulleh Shah, the great Punjabi poet who says, "Destroy the mosque, destroy the temple, destroy anything that can be destroyed. But be careful with the human heart, because it is in the human heart where God can reside." This is Bulleh Shah riffing off the *hadith qudsi* (extra-Quranic revelation) that "The Universe cannot contain Me, but the heart of My believing servant can."

I'm less concerned about the art that the artist produces. We can analyze it, we can talk about the *halal*ness or the *haram*ness of it, about whether it fits into the tradition. But what really worries me are those who crush human hearts. And there are many in our communities, many who call themselves religious scholars, who use their traditions to crush human hearts, instead of nurturing them.

For Abdal-Hayy, being a Muslim was all about being present in everything we do. To bring all parts of ourselves to our faith and service. Islam absorbs, it accepts and embraces all of us. Abdal-Hayy believed that. His life and work are testimony to it.

Art shows us where we're at in this messy now. Abdal-Hayy showed us poetry that was outside the rigid metrics of "classical poetry." His was mostly poetry without meter, that scoffed at convention, set aside form. It was poetry that smashed words together and gave us stanzas that appeared like a Big Bang and settled into beautiful constellations. We must celebrate this craft, this art. That's why this book is important.

Abdal-Hayy left us an extraordinary corpus. Poetry by Muslim writers, particularly women and women of color, is changing the very field of poetry. When I hear this new, challenging, and beautiful work, I want Abdal-Hayy to be in the room. I want to imagine what conversations he would have with these new and emerging poets. What advice would he give them? What would they disagree on? On what matters would they find common ground?

We need to have a space where our Muslim poetics can be explored on their own terms. Where the output isn't policed or obliged to pass some test of authenticity. Culture isn't static. It's organic. And it includes everyone. The field of poetry should be open, a place where people can bring the whole of themselves, where we can celebrate the things that God has made incredibly complex. In a time where we are all witness to injustice, violence, pain, and trauma, we need the poets the most.

Cultural leadership today is as important as political leadership, and – I would say – as important as religious leadership. That may not be a popular sentiment in some quarters, but the time for caring is long gone. The hour is late. The world is beautiful and difficult, joyful and sad, painful and full of drama. I think we just need to speak truth first to ourselves. If there's anything that Abdal-Hayy can teach us, it's that he was speaking the truth to himself all the time. There's so much healing in that.

Abdal-Hayy gave all of us an inheritance. It's not some rarefied thing that only some of the poets can have access to. These words are for everyone. They deserve to be studied. They need to be part of our cultural and literary education.

I believe that Abdal-Hayy's legacy is alive. I'm thankful that this book has been published. It will help keep that legacy accessible and known. The generations to come will regard Abdal-Hayy as he should be regarded – one of the great poets of this land. His work will be referential. This volume is just the beginning. There is much to be written, created, inspired by the poems herein. And when the day comes that we enter the Garden Eternal, I have no doubt that Abdal-Hayy will be there composing verse, strumming his zither, rushing to make us tea. He will remain in *Firdaus* what he was in life – extraordinary.

It was an honor to know him. I love and miss you, Sidi. Till the day that friend is joined with friend.

ABDUL-REHMAN MALIK
*New Haven, Connecticut*
*September 2021*

# BIOGRAPHY

Berkeley, CA, 1970: A young Beat poet by the name of Daniel Moore was causing a sensation in the Counterculture scene with his poetry, not to mention his faux fur-covered Chevy with deer antlers on the hood, Astroturf carpeting the floor, and a toadstool for a driver's seat.

Where do you go after you've rubbed shoulders with Allen Ginsberg and Michael McClure, and had your debut collection of poems published by Lawrence Ferlinghetti of the legendary City Lights Bookstore in San Francisco? For several years Daniel had visited gurus, sat in *zazen* with Zen teacher Shunryu Suzuki, practiced yoga every morning, and led a "sacred theater" troupe, The Floating Lotus Magic Opera Company, complete with handmade puppets, skull necklaces, drums, flutes, and lots of long, wavy hair.

This circle of avant-garde artists – who saw Daniel as a kind of spiritual leader – didn't just want to shake up the turgid American psyche of the time with their eclectic amalgam of shamanism, Zen and Tibetan Buddhism, and Hinduism, as seen through acid-tinted glasses. Their lofty ambition was, in fact, to exorcize America's demons of violence and war. Several public performances earned them an article in *Rolling Stone* magazine in February 1970, which says:

"The shaping spirit of the Floating Lotus company is a lion-maned poet named Daniel Moore... Though he exerts himself to make the opera a collective product, through group meditation at rehearsals, continual rewriting and the interaction of living closely with the actors, it is necessarily deeply stamped with his spirit. It is poetic, rather than a dramatic stage..."

A copy of this magazine wound its way to the terrace of the celebrated expat hangout, the Paris Café in Tangiers, where a Scotsman by the name of Ian Dallas was reading it. An American sitting at the next table noticed the picture of Daniel, leaned over, and commented that he knew him.

Dallas asked politely for Daniel's number. It turned out that Dallas had recently returned from a visit to the *zawiyah* (Sufi lodge) of the great Moroccan Sufi, Shaykh Muhammad Ibn al-Habib, where he had embraced Islam, taking the name Abdalqadir, and been made a *Muqaddim* ("one who brings forward;" a kind of deputy) of the Darqawiyya-Habibiyya order.

As a cultural influencer who might inspire others to follow suit, Daniel seemed like a natural person with whom to share this spiritual path. As it happened, that year Daniel had come across R.A. Nicholson's translation of Mevlana Jalaluddin Rumi's Mathnawi and taken to giving impromptu readings in the hallway of the large Victorian house where he lived, where he was busy typing up a new poetry manuscript in his temple-like attic room.

Arriving in Berkeley, Abdalqadir went straight to the artist commune and Daniel's garret, where he proceeded to regale him with vivid depictions of Islam and the saint he had so recently seen. Daniel was captivated:

"For the three days following our meeting, two other Americans and I listened in awe as this magnificent storyteller unfolded the picture of Islam, of the perfection of the Prophet Muhammad ﷺ, and of the 100-year-old-plus Shaykh, sitting under a great fig tree in a garden with his disciples, singing praises of Allah.

"It was everything I'd always dreamed of. It was poetry come alive. It was the visionary experience made part of daily life, with the Prophet a perfectly balanced master of wisdom and simplicity, an historically accessible Buddha, with a mixture of the earthiness of Moses, the otherworldliness of Jesus, and a light all his own."

The same year, Daniel made a trip to Meknes for the annual Moussem gathering in homage to the saint Sidi Muhammad Ibn Al-Habib, where he was given the name 'Abdal-Hayy, formally accepted the *tariqa* (Sufi order), and committed to help establish it in the US. Over the next few years he was involved in several *zawiyah*s in Berkeley, where a small but enthusiastic group of converts converged.

About this time, Abdal-Hayy[1] was advised by Abdalqadir to desist from writing, as he was perhaps doing it "obsessively" – advice he followed

---

1    Among several possible renderings into Latin script, this was the spelling that Abdal-Hayy preferred.

for almost a decade. Meanwhile, he recognised that the *wird* (litany) of his Shaykh that he was reciting twice daily and his *diwan* (poetry collection), which they sang at their nightly *dhikr* sessions, were having a formative impact on his understanding of poetry. In them, he writes, he "...saw poetry in its true function as a joining of beauty with truth. Here was poetry that had a spiritual reality to lead its reader or reciter (or singer) to enlightenment (and connecting to my earlier interest in sacred texts), as a vehicle for knowledge of Allah...to know Him by His multifarious manifestations on earth and in the heavens."

During this time, Abdal-Hayy lived and traveled throughout Spain, the UK, Algeria, Morocco, and Nigeria, and helped edit Aisha and Abdal-Haqq Bewley's new translation of the Qur'an into English. He landed in Santa Barbara, CA, in the early 1980s, where he once again began to write poetry; as his wife Malika describes it, "the floodgates opened."

In keeping with Abdal-Hayy's myriad fascinations, encyclopedic poetic references, and wholehearted drive to know and honor Truth in all its disclosures, the poetry that poured out was rich in cosmic imagery, sprinkled with gazelles and zebras and geese flying overhead, but also made tangible with street scenes, vernacular references, and tender vignettes of family life. It is a deeply personal prayer, proof positive that love of Allah can be expressed in any language and that the "signs on the horizons" are to be found in the most everyday and surprising of places.

Another aspect of Abdal-Hayy's diverse artistic output was puppetry. He used several home-made puppets in Floating Lotus performances, and in fact funded his travels to Europe and Morocco by putting on musical puppet shows together with two other members of the Floating Lotus troupe, Conrad and Susan Archuletta.

Later, Abdal-Hayy's puppets would be a great source of entertainment for his children and grandchildren. In 2000, Abdal-Hayy wrote a rhyme-and-verse play about Layla and Majnun, based on the classical poem by Nizami, which he performed several times in New York and Philadelphia, using puppets that he and his wife Malika made themselves.

The same year, Abdal-Hayy was commissioned by the Lotus Music & Dance studio – founded by another former member of Floating Lotus,

Kamala Cesar – to write and perform a piece of poetry entitled "The New York Ramayana."

The following year, Kamala – a member of the Mohawk Nation – commissioned him to write, direct, and narrate a piece of theater entitled *The Eagle Dance: A tribute to the Mohawk high-steel workers*, about the Mohawk "Skywalkers," high-steel workers who worked on New York skyscrapers, including the World Trade Center. The production was initially canceled due to the tragic events of 9/11, but it was later performed several times.

Abdal-Hayy would also become poetry editor for *Islamica Magazine* and Zaytuna College's *Seasons* journal, as well as editor for the translations into English of the work of Palestinian poet Mahmoud Darwish, and Hamza Yusuf's translation of the *Burda of Imam al-Busiri*, among other titles.

In 2011, 2012, and 2014, Abdal-Hayy won a Nazim Hikmet Prize for Poetry, and in 2013 he won an American Book Award, for *Blood Songs*. In 2013, and 2014, he was listed among The 500 Most Influential Muslims for his poetry.

Daniel Abdal-Hayy Moore continued writing daily, and prolifically, until he was no longer able to hold a pen. After patiently bearing with cancer for five years, he passed away peacefully on April 18th 2016, رحمه الله, and was buried at the Bawa Muhaiyaddeen Fellowship Farm, located in East Fallowfield, Pennsylvania.

When Kelly Abdal-Lateef Hayden came to collect his body for burial, he found Abdal-Hayy's right index finger raised in representation of his *shahada* (witnessing Divine Oneness). Not long after his burial, some of those present recall that the clouds had been transfigured into pearlescent rainbows.

MEDINA TENOUR WHITEMAN
*Órgiva, Spain*
*September 2021*

# NOTE ON THE SELECTION

Daniel Abdal-Hayy Moore authored over sixty manuscripts, so making a selection of his poems has been no easy task. Initially we had intended to include only forty, but this proved impossible, as there were too many must-reads that we felt would be excluded.

A number of Abdal-Hayy's poems have been well-loved for several decades now, and these were our natural starting point. However, within his seemingly inexhaustible oeuvre, it is gratifying to stumble occasionally upon some as-yet unacknowledged gem, so this was our opportunity to bring these to a wider audience, too.

We have tried to select poems that express the full array of spiritual and literary influences in Abdal-Hayy's life, as well as the range of his favorite themes, without over-representing any one of them.

However, he wrote extensively about two topics in particular: fasting and death. Anyone who wishes to read more on these topics is referred to *Ramadan Sonnets* and *Ramadan Is Burnished Sunlight*; and *Down at the Deep End*, *The Sweet Enigma of It All*, *Transitioning to Zero*, and *Holy Door in the Ground*, respectively.

In keeping with the poet's personal tradition, wherever possible we have cited the date on which each poem was written, adding the name of the collection in which it originally appeared (where applicable) for reference. A list of his complete works can be found at the back of the book.

Throughout several of his last books, Abdal-Hayy merely numbered his poems; they have been presented here with titles taken from the first line.

When organising the poems into categories, we have borne in mind readers who ask for poems for particular occasions, such as marriages or Mawlid; poems about animals (another of Abdal-Hayy's go-to metaphors); or humorous poems. We hope these groupings make it easy for readers to find poems on specific themes.

Arranging these poems into categories has been a challenge as many dealt with several topics at once; "Talk," for instance, could well be in the Animals

& Nature category, or in Signs of Allah. Likewise, both "Adam's Indelible Imprint" and "Adam Stood in the World" relate not only to Prophets but also to fasting.

Ultimately, all of Abdal-Hayy's poems are a kind of *dhikr*, a remembrance of Allah. We have tried to place each poem where we felt it shone best, and welcome conversations around what they are really about.

M.T.W.

SELECTED POEMS

---

*Heart Wisdom*

# A BRAVE AND RUINED MAN

A brave and ruined man
became a sudden flying bird
whose wingspread spanned the
skies

He closed his eyes in a crowded
room and a chorus of voices
trembled through his fluttering
voice that drew water from
invisible wells and spun
honey from invisible hives

*Salaams* from a shore
beyond water and an ocean
beyond waves

A sky leans down and takes
us up by our hands to draw us
up


November 2013, #28, *He Comes Running*

# THE HEART IS A WHITE BOWL

The heart is a white bowl of fresh
    sweet peaches set in the
windowsill in the sunlight.

The head is a slow nod
in the direction of Truth.

The body is a highway in a
Third World country in
constant need of repair.

The soul is an endless measure of moonlight.

The soul is a white spot in a black field.

The soul is a black spot in a white field.

The soul is a green estuary in a
    shadowy area.

I stand up inside the
shadow of the soul.

I look out through the eyes of
    no one.

The seeing is God's
What is seen by His Seeing
is visible proof of His existence.

The sunlight the white
bowl of fresh peaches sits in.

The white bowl of peaches,

and the ray of yellow sunlight in which
the white bowl of peaches sits.


3/19/1996, *The Blind Beekeeper*

## NOT A MOMENT

Not a moment can be squandered
not a moment can be lost

Grab the rope and swing out
over the abyss

*"What rope?"* you say
when there are

ropes all around us

dangling at our elbows and lying in
coils at our feet

But invisible to our visible eyes

Our eyes must quit the visible
to see them

They swing in frayed joyance
between visible trees

and if grabbing them proves problematic
just leap in their direction

and you'll catch the catch that catches you
the rope that love flings

*What am I saying?* No

rope no trees no cliffs

No abyss

but *this!*

Our heart's enough to take us
to the goal

Our hearts surround
incalculable bliss


1/13/2009, *Stretched Out on Amethysts*

## BE KIND

Be kind to your shoes
it's not their fault your

feet hurt and miss slipping
into them the first time in the

dark

Be kind to the others at the
table who may be hungrier than

you though they may also be
observant of your needs

Be kind to soap that can only
last so long frothing off your

superficial grime

Be kind to sound that goes
everywhere at once and strikes ears

waiting for the call or simply
sensitive to noise

Be kind to the sun that
appears at our horizon as we

tilt toward it swinging
around it whistling as we

go

Essentially kindness is an elixir
that turns rock to gold hard

hearts to running streams

and is enshrined deeply engraved on
mystic tablets just inside

the shadow of the cave

Every creature shows kindness
when it's not afraid

Flakes falling through the air are kind

Ourselves falling
as we die


4/23/2010, *In Constant Incandescence*

## FORGIVENESS

Forgiveness is a doorway of light in a
  dark building in the
    worst part of town,

it's a globule of nectar dripped
  down from an exotic flower that
blooms only once each year on an
    ice-glittery Himalayan peak,

it's a herd of new lambs appearing
  miraculously to the nomadic tribe
    suffering from drought.

Forgiveness is the victim's mother
looking into the eyes of the accused and saying,
*"The sky is so blue, every tiny forget-me-not
    is bathed in its light."*

Forgiveness is the current in the
  electric chair turning into
    choirs of angels, singing a
  single high note celestially
    over and over.

Forgiveness is the prodigal son or daughter
  returning home to the agéd parents
    with scars and beatitudes
and not a word spoken of the disappearance,
the table is set, the steaming
    food set down, the
      glasses filled.

Forgiveness is a field of wildflowers
    burst into bloom like flames,
illuminating the face of the estranged,
it's the sound of tubas at the
    bottom of a well, the
sound of a beloved's voice after years of strife,

it's a neon Yes after blackout nights of No,
it's the heart weeping a thousand
    years of tears until the
exhausted body around it
    is renewed, gets up,

turns on a faucet whose running water
whispers, *"I forgive you,"*
the tears are brushed back and
the face becomes the
    face of the full moon,
bright saffron in the night

in the heat of a Philadelphia summer
        bathed in quiet.


6/22/1997, *Chants for the Beauty Feast*

## TALK

Talk to your body
talk to your soul

Talk to the thunder on the hill

Talk to God's world in
which we dwell

the day in tumult
the night that's still

Talk to creatures that
cross your path

lambs of peace
Tygers of wrath

The door that's shut
the door that's open

If we talk to God's world
we talk to God

Who's the only One Who
makes things happen

They say one went mad
talking to roses

but in their beauty
saw God's responses

The sunset pouring its
gold in the sky

filled his heart
as it filled his eye

and as he talked to the
air around him

The Friend found him


7/13/2012, *Down at the Deep End*

## PIECE OF COAL

The piece of coal that wanted to be diamond
   said to the earth: *Press me.*

The succulent grape that wanted to be wine
   said to the feet: *Crush me.*

The cloud that wanted to be thunder and rain
   said to a facing cloud: *Collide with me.*

The mountain that wanted to be level valley
   said to the elements: *Erode me.*

The oyster that wanted to produce a pearl
   said to a sand-grain: *Irritate me.*

The heart that wanted to be filled with light
   said to the world: *Break me.*


2/12/1996, *The Blind Beekeeper* (extract)

The Imaginal World

## ROUND EARTH

I have this sensation that
    walking on the earth
I'm walking on the top of a ball,

walking on the sidewalk after dusk with a
quart of raw milk just purchased from the
        Co-op

I'm on the round top of a ball
swimming straight along in the night,

earth-green globe, wind-curling Whitmanesque
silhouette of Brahms strolling by a fence

on the curve of a hill, the whole
spinning slowly enough that

everything thinks it's on the top curve
rather than the bottom, trees

wave their leaves in the
breeze as they
spin past, crickets

hunker down in the
grass to hum their monotonous sonatas,

things fly off the curve as it
slides by in the
    grease of space, then fall

back on it again as if it were the
    most natural thing to do, monarch

butterflies twittering their orange-black
    wings as they
        flutter down, leap of

mongoose gone after
        cobra, flying squirrel who somehow

calculates its
    fall to land
        exactly in
            place as the
ball spins under it,

fish underwater the
    coziest of all, as they

        slosh in the bowl that
            swings like a slow

        lamp in the
            night, the whole rolling

earth on its
spherical wheel having been

placed here by Perfection in the most

balanced of atmospheres, with a

perfect spin and cen-
        trifugal motion to keep us all

dancing until
    death slows us
        down to a

    standstill at last, the

ball

continuing to roll

under us

like a lion

perpetually

crouched to leap

through the

opening in the trees of the

stars but

never does.


9/24/1987, *Exploratory Odes*

# THE HEART CAME OUT OF THE BODY

The heart came out of the body
and spoke and by heart we mean
that living forest of swinging birds
and musical knowledge interwoven
among leaves of ancient trees

By the heart we mean the heart
of the heart which is a boundless
ocean waiting for the touch of God
to illumine under the brightest sky

By heart what is meant is what
already knows the truth the
way trees know how to grow

When the singer began to sing a
voice from far away came up
through his throat where many
drunk dervishes have vanished
and reappeared


November 2013, #27, *He Comes Running*

# A SCIENTIST WALKED INTO A WALL

A scientist walked into a
wall and broke his nose

A theologian walked into a
wall and

became the wall

A saint saw no wall at
all

He saw only Allah on
both sides of the

wall he saw not at all

and the rising and the
falling like a

galloping horse's back

and the circular seasons
descending and ascending

like the throbs in a
bloodstream

and the fish in it swimming
oceanward


12/19/2016, #18, *Transitioning to Zero*

## A LITTLE BLUE MONK

A little blue monk in a purple
cassock served us sarsaparilla

He looked through eyes that had been
through a thousand years of blinking

I think to him we resembled chrysanthemums
in coloured vases

He wept as he told us his joys
and how the light irradiated his little

cell at night and how soft the
voices and deep the import

A faqir came along in a yellow djallaba
and brought tame giraffes to ride

"These are swifter than most and one
bound takes us to the far horizon

to the rising or setting sun – whichever
you wish"

We rode all day and the sun rose
successively for love was in the

air and nothing could stop us from

diving right into it and through its
heartfelt syrups

A little Buddha appeared and held his
hand above his head to indicate we'd

arrived at the right location

for his feet knew each terrain as perfect
and he knew for us what was

perfect for our feet as well
as we looked out over the sheerest

canyons for miles and miles we'd
ever seen

and from the depths of their crevasses rose
colored streamers and

rays of golden light

and the voices here assured us we'd
arrived at the appropriate place

When we looked around there was
no one there but we were

not alone

and a Face of Light floated in the
air in front of us

to show us our souls


6/3/2012, *Down at the Deep End*

## THE AUTHOR'S VOICE

I opened a book to read
and the text spoke to me
   in the author's voice!
Roomfuls of Italian marble statues
rolled their eyes toward me as I
      passed.
A cube of air opened up one of its
   sides in space, and I
entered. I'm
   sailing in it now. Incandescent.
Over the sea. Waves below as if a
   medieval beast were churning.
A medieval
   beast is churning. Lanterns have
a trapped djinn in them.
Flames shoot and spurt. Someone
opened their bedroom door the other day
and a dozen pure white
   horses galloped out at full
      steam, silvery manes
         streaming.
Things have changed. I sat in the
damp room and opened the
   book on my lap. The great binding
creaked. As soon as the
   pages lay flat
the text started speaking
   in the author's voice!
I opened book after book. Page after
page fell open and the
   author's own distinct
voice could be heard.

I opened the Qur'an.
*Holy! Holy! Holy!*
Trees on the hill
   burst into flame!
The stairway became a
   graduated hierarchy
     of blue pools!
Outside the window the
   sky turned black
behind a rush of white doves!
Holy Voice so loving
went straight to my heart!
Direct Voice of
   He Who
created the fishes and
   the clouds.
The Voice from the page
   entered me.
If I listen real close to
   silence I can hear it.
If I bend down into myself
I can hear His Voice speaking.


11/3/1995, *The Angel Broadcast* (unpublished manuscript)

Animals & Nature

# HOME FOR THE OWL

Home for the owl is a high tree bough,
home for a mouse is a deep-down hole,
home for a man is his hopes and fears
but his deepest home is Allah.

Honeybees store their pollen in hives,
spiders store their food in webs,
man holds everything close to his heart
but his deepest heart is Allah.

If a bird flies far it knows its way home,
salmon fight fierce rapids upstream,
when we leave on a trip we know its end
but its true end is always Allah.

We end where we began, in the middle of the world,
in the center of our universe of love and pain,
we never venture far from the center of our being
but its center is only Allah.


2/4/1998, *You Open a Door and It's a Starry Night*

# THE SOUND OF GEESE OVER THE HOUSE

The sound of geese over the house

and in the house the prayer on the Prophet

The sound of geese over the house

and in the house Allah loves you

The mountains are full of light and their
gigantic shadows are eloquent since they're
leaning against the sky and out in space with their
crags and outcrops

No sound can scale in a dimension commensurate with
the pure expanse of it

The sound of geese over the house

puts a dome of life above us and a
sea of life below us and a
world of life all around us

and a shaft of living Light inside us


6/21/2007, *The Sound of Geese over the House*

# THE WHITE DEER

It's even closer than our fingertips
what we're longing for
and travel for in search of
closer than our jugular

Shangri La lies languorously
always out of reach
its silver trays heaped high with
succulence its windows basking in
perennial sunlight

Darkness wraps thc dearness of the
depth we fathom but not distance
and the rhythm of it singing in our
eardrums brings it even closer to us

Can't call it can't name it
loss is often the way toward it
less is often more in its regard
as we face the chalk snow always
falling across it

And make the face that was ours before birth
come alive in our eyes then our
nose and mouth and the rest
as if clouds were evaporating away from it
leaving it clear

See the white deer standing so close
on the shore bending to drink then
standing still head held high
before leaping away

its reflection in the water writing in
silvery light our most secret name His
answer to our deepest call?

A moon lightens the picture
and where it was a moment ago
fills with light
I can't explain why the journey takes us
to the place it does
only to find it's taken us to our
starting place

A ball of concentrated matter
tightens itself to a point
that speeds through space so fast
it goes nowhere is nowhere then is
all and we liken our destiny to its
fall but it doesn't fall

I can't explain why that tiny point soon
covers us over all or
why as we age we haven't gone
anywhere at all

The white deer bounds through the end of space
faster than light can follow her
and comes up in front of us again to drink
our blood's clear nectar

Sweet as a vapor trail
flicking its deer's tail
as we also disappear to be more
tangible to ourselves after all

Closer in a mysterious visibility
to our initial caul[2]


1/28/2003, *Psalms for the Brokenhearted*

---

2    Caul (noun): the amniotic membrane enclosing a fetus.

# WHO TAUGHT WHO WHAT

The eagle taught the rabbit
 how to keep out of sight.

The bear taught the trout
 how to slip away.

The elephant taught its mahout
 how to scrub its back.

The dwarf taught the growing boy
 how to look tall.

The window taught the wall
 how to be more transparent.

The floor taught the roof
 how to be more down to earth.

The water taught the wine
 how to be always clear-headed.

The wine taught the water
 how to throw off all restraints.

The earth taught the blind man
 how to see with his feet.

The wind taught the toupee
 how to be more truthful.

The rainbow taught our hearts
 how to expect more of the unseen.

The bridge taught the river
   how to overcome obstacles.

The mule taught the townspeople
   how to put up with its braying.

The lovers taught each other
   how to accept each other's faults.

Darkness taught daylight
   how to wait until it's time.

The body taught the soul
   not to rely on it forever.


11/20/1997, *You Open a Door and It's a Starry Night*

## SOME LEAVES FALL

*for Mohja Kahf*

Some leaves fall spiraling down.
Some leaves fall lopsidedly zigzagedly down.
Some seem to fall like plummets straight down.
Some twist and spin as they fall down.
Some seem to take their sweet time sailing down.
Detach themselves, fall through the air, land at our
     feet, from their treetop heights,
bronze and dry, down, down,

falling through the morning air, crisp clear
October air, crisp golden petal-like leaves
showering individually down,
some at a rakish slant,
some tumbling acrobatically down,
little leaves Galileoly racing big ones down,
all adding mulch to the glittery forest floor,
however they came down,

awed me, catching my breath as I see ones as if
     for me especially
falling right in front of my eyes, however
     mathematically calculable their
fall, making a
   spectacularly humble finale

down.


10/26/1998, *Some*

# IRIS

In the silence of the forest floor
a single iris rises.
In the forests of the entire earth
we always find surprises,
a light shaft from the redwood's peak,
a dark bog full of frogs,
white owls fluffing feathers,
termites hollowing logs.

Variety runs through us, joining,
elements in rings,
there is a song of unity
that choirs through all earth's things.

But we go beyond to where the song
is elevated past our eyes,
it's there the meaning comes
where all intentions rise
beyond the heaviness of flesh
to show the reality of our acts,
and in the next world's light supreme
in new light lay the facts
of our quick life. No dream
but this one where we move,
this one where we live and die,
then the world of pure light opens up
and into it we fly

as we never flew before
through death's door.

1984, *previously unpublished*

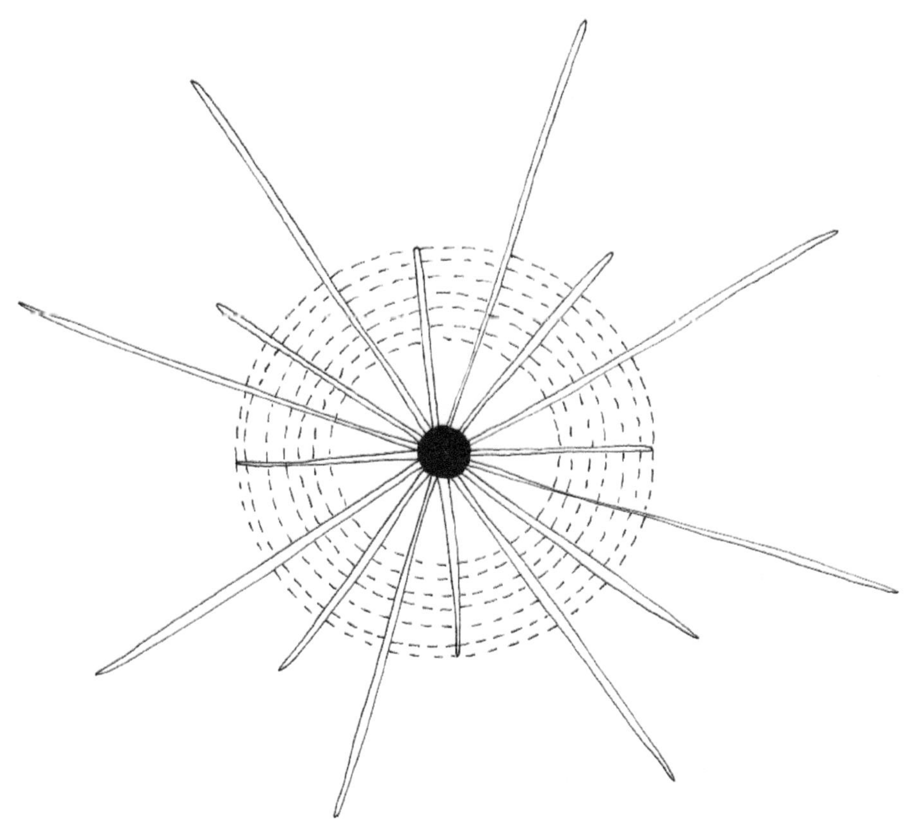

*Light in the Darkness*

# WHAT HAVE WE GOT

At five o'clock in the morning after the
Morning Prayer on the
    first day of two weeks'
        notice of being "let go" from my
job of eight years because they
can't afford to pay me any more, what have I
        got? Dear Lord,
You. First.
Foremost. This
    earth a
tiny place. The
heart holds all.

Five senses, light-filled near
    clock-tick, distant
    car-swish, this early. Dark outside.

I've got wife, blue and
    starry skies shining
        silver behind her when she
embraces me and says she's
    with me no matter
        what, and she also
her own world's proof and truth.
Our children
    guaranteed blessing of provision by their
very souls' existence in our
    living domain, their
sustenance
    written for them from
before eternity, it comes in material form through

thick and thin, seeking them
    out. And

they themselves
    stutter forward in
growth-spurts on the
    chronological movie, joy in their
surprise consciousness, their
    own beings throwing out
        unique lights casting
twelve-dimensional shadows in broad daylight
against the air.

And I've been
in and out of the earth, up and
    down on it, and
keep arriving
back to this point, actually
landing upright, Lord, Lord, after
any upsets, retrievable
    miles unrollable inside of
more highway into dark wilderness, that
    ends up in
        familiar
            territory each
                time,

and this love of writing it down,
that maybe its
aroma remind somebody casually passing under my
    window,

and, my God, my window given at
    birth, window

till death, same
window beyond, our
    windows, each of us has
    to see through, reach
through, breathe steam on the
glass pane to write out Your

    Infinite Name.


6/22/1989, *Facing Mecca* (extract)

# THE TURNS WE TAKE

the turns we take
that turn upon us

the roads we take
that fall upon us

the knobs we turn
to pass through

the tales we tell
that aren't true

how one turn
deserves another

that may turn out
to be one smoother

or rougher
how what doesn't

kill us makes us
tougher

that we end in
joy and laughter

instead of heart's
disaster

before His Divine
Face

that faces us before
and after

2016, #25, *Holy Door in the Ground*

## A THOUSAND ARCHERS

A thousand archers stationed behind walls,
a thousand pistols facing us from behind doors,
potholes in the asphalt the size of moon craters,
stepladders with loose steps one step alone will dislodge,
huge fists with comic book starbursts around them
  heading our way,
trains bearing down on us tied to the tracks, sweaty and
  apprehensive,
great balls of fire heading toward us from outer space,
calamity in the financial market, disaster on the
  domestic front,
earthquake, jaws of two sides of an earth-rift
   opening right under us, swallowing us
    whole,
our plaintive cries lost in the night, our echoing
cries down stairwells or between redwood trees tall as
Saturn, our bewildered persons on a planet the
  size of a pea in a
universe the size of the Sahara a billion times over,

all of it closing in, closing in all around these
bodies of ours as our mortality laps at us like the
waters of terrific oceans until our
natural barriers can no longer bear it, and
  burst,
starlight upon us, endless Milky Way trails
  blistering the blackness with
snow-twinkle, Lord, all these

actual adversities against us, and
You Sovereign over all, calm
Voice in the darkness, deep

Light in the darkness, Beautiful
Face in the darkness, Your

Light in the darkness.


5/30/1998, #4, *Salt Prayers*

## THEY TRY TO APPROACH

They try to approach with explosives
but the Throne of Allah stays

implacably still
radiating its concern

The silence of the sky is not His
lack of articulation

but one of the salient features
of His Speech

If a window goes up and
someone leans out

where before there was no one
does that mean that until then the

building was empty?

I want a river of jubilation
and the camel driver's

endless song

Storming heaven was
never a good idea

A mother suckling her young
knows the truth of its intimate

location
be it human woman or doe

on her nest of pine needles on a
forest floor

They try to rattle the windows when
no one's there with

hand grenades

But He Who Sees it all in one glance
has already nodded His approval or

displeasure before the
dust settles

and the pain that rips through the
human body

is the harsh song of God's rebuke

*Come*

Approach it as you would
a stern superior

and watch love's waters
flood toward you


2/11/2012, *The Match That Becomes a Conflagration*

## A LITTLE RAMSHACKLE SHACK

A little ramshackle shack on a hill
blown apart by the wind
door roof and walls lofted aloft and sent flying
no weightier than paper upon which is casually written
a name
twists in the air almost signals goodbye then
suddenly is gone only
bare hillside left behind
a goat now stands upon
two goats a small herd after the wind's died down
straggle along distractedly
chewing

*

This is the music space
where music is most difficult
this place of joy and horror
sound of fuselage entering steel as if

slicing through butter

This is the silence out of which
all the thrilling chords emerge

This is the space of the silence of souls
at their moment of release

This is the air over a dewy wheatfield
crackling like cellophane in the morning light

This is the music space
voices in a room of those
visible and those who are invisible

I think the music of the spheres
can be heard in this space

It's the sound of life
which takes place without echo

or is nothing but echo

And the original sound is the
sound of God alone audible to Himself
and we are the humming elements of that sound

This is the music space
we hear it this very moment

It's the sound of hooves
and nothing at all like the sound of hooves

It's the endlessly heaving ocean-sound
which turns out to be our blood beating
and the deep tidal push of our own heartbeats

Each whisper of love and fear and grief
rises in this music space

And one single note is enough to fill it

and silence itself is part of it

and the silence or the sound that follows it
is also part of it


9/15-16/2001, *The Music Space* (extract)[3]

---

3   Written in New York after 9/11 and read at a memorial at St Peter's cathedral in
    New York.

# TYRANTS DRIVE PAST STATUES OF THEMSELVES

Tyrants are fleeing their countries in
    black limousines
driving past statues of themselves
huddled in back seats, counting
        on anonymity,

driving past statues of themselves
    erected during their salad days,
hoping against hope to get to the borders unrecognized,
their last days of iron-fisted action
backfired, explosions bouncing back
like repeated radio broadcasts
        in their hectic brains,

their loyal armies shooting into shouting crowds of comrades
backfiring until
giant shouting comrade-crowds fill palace doorways
            demanding
                    tyrant blood

who now flee by back roads, at night, in
black limousines

driving past statues of themselves.


12/23/1989, *A Maddening Disregard for the Passage of Time*[4]

---

4    Written during the execution of Romanian dictator Nicolae Ceauçescu and his
     wife Elena.

# I'M MORE CONCERNED

I'm more concerned
I'm more concerned he said
of how these next few years
these next few years will affect the small and

perishable things that dare to poke their
poke their heads up through the
permafrost that confronts us all that
confronts the big and small as we

battle against the very inertia that drowned
the unconcerned of Noah's time of the very old
time of Noah who very
successfully unsuccessfully built the

boat but failed to save his
people who were too busy being unimaginative though all
though all the signs were there for them
to see

the small and brave of us as well as the
big and strong

facing the wall of water
the mile-high wall of water that's just now on the
brink of cresting and rushing down with all its

absolutely every ounce of its impact wondering what
hit us

as if the earth itself were raised like a
wrecking ball and swung against itself

shattering the continents and splashing the
seas into space like a dog shaking itself

like a dog bounding onto the shore from a cascading
rush of water and
shaking itself dry


2/16/2000, *Shaking the Quicksilver Pool*

# HERE'S THE WINDOW

Here's the window you
can't climb out of

Here's the banquet you
cannot eat

Here's the sunlight that
showers another world

Here's the life you can't
repeat

Tigers each side of the
road you travel

hungrier than time
to swiftly devour you

You can't avoid them so
don't even try

Those who survive them
are very few

The key is held in the
hand of a saint

One turn in the lock is
all it takes

But how to turn it you
must be taught

somewhere between hope and
deep heartbreaks

The less you become the
greater you are

Shaving down is no
easy task

Have heart without ceasing
alone in the universe

The answer comes each
time you ask

The door won't open so
don't bother knocking

Your soul dwells already on
the other side

Go through yourself as
through a door

and in God's Light and
Grace abide


4/21/2014, *The Sweet Enigma of It All*

## THE WELL

Some days there's a well at the
bottom of my garden and
some days there's none

A bucket appears in the air I'm
allowed to let down

A golden rope is attached that
shines in the sun

When I pull the bucket back up
it's full of milk

Moonlight shines in the milk
and makes it silver

If you drink the milk you become
a version of the original

Your hand shows the landscape
your heart wants to reside in

The bucket's let down in the dark
where shadows dwell

In the shadows are moving shapes
and occasionally speech

The air gets crowded with presences
asking for space

When you drink the milk time and
space get effaced

I call out to you from a
place far away

I see God's angels streaming down to
earth with messages

Our singing can never reach
their intensity of song

A length of rope is let down
into the dark

Let the light anoint the
hand of your fate with its laughter

Your weeping will cease
and you'll be made lighter

Some days there's no well
at the bottom of my garden

But I hear its bucket
hit the sides and splash in the darkness

The echo of it rings in my ears
and my heart strains to listen

God is nearer than our jugular vein
we're the far ones

Let the bucket down slowly
its golden rope will serve you

Delicious silvery milk
is the resulting secret

There's so much light everywhere
it begins to hurt a little

Let God's light allow
every other light to be lit

Some days a well appears
some days not

When it doesn't appear we praise its source
when it does we become it

Let God's voice allow the light
to surface

Moon and sunlight
glitter on its shining surface

When we lean in to see
a face appears that's not our face

It's not a face at all
it's a version of the original

I don't think the well will appear again
and then it's there

My job is to wait and listen
and keep the garden clear

Your job O God is
to fill us with wonder


4/5/2003, *Psalms for the Brokenhearted*

Signs of Allah

## SIGNS OF ALLAH

When the tide of the day pulls out and
leaves the night standing on the shore

swallowing the stars

and the moon is nearly halfway to
completing its luminous shell

and the night stretches its arms to
expand as far as the

globe's curvature will allow
with the sun's spotlight lighting up where

night is not and the night
darkening to the hazy line between them

and we take all this into our
bodies with the daytime fast

are we not now inhabiting a space that is
neither exactly terrestrial nor celestial

but by the decree of prophetic consciousness
participating as we might otherwise not

in the in and out breathing of Allah's most
essential creating?

We see the signs of Allah on the
horizons of heaven and earth

and they are

ourselves


8/14/2011, 14 Ramadan, *Ramadan Is Burnished Sunlight*

## NAME OF GOD

The Name of God came haunting down the hall
and dazzled all our eyes and ears and
   hearts, and made us

swoon into this hard physical life,
and we'll be wakened and called back

and then we'll leave this world as
things departing from shadows
leave their shadows in heaps like
   old clothes at the
      door

through which we'll all depart to go back to that
chanting school, those corridors of
   pure reverberation through

pine woods, mountain cloud, egrets hovering in an
   updraft, sunlight on
      rock, sun twinkle on

stream gush, that exquisite

Name of God again, repeated by God's own
speech on the tongue of everything.

The Name of God foghorns
   out at sea where
blackened darkness deepens within darkness.

The Name of God suspended in amoebas hovering just below the
   surface tension of a moonlit lake.

The Name of God in the first movements of an eaglet inside its high shell on
a cliff beaten by
    wind, its brother and sister eaglets
        starting to stretch inside
their shells at exactly the
            same time.
The Name of God in the high wind beating against them.

The Name of God in rigging out at sea
    the high wind beats against.
The Name of God in the audible beats that
    accompany the wind, in the
silent beats as well as the
ones sounded out, the lapping as well as the
    silence as the sea recedes.

Laughter followed by the silence of death.

The Name of God in them both.


9/21/2003, *Chants for the Beauty Feast* (extract)

# TOUCHSTONE

The touchstone here
is any who hears the name of Allah
turns to gold
or in the case of the heart
a river

A sapling becomes a
tree in an instant
the eye
a seer centuries old
or in the case of the greedy
a giver

He suffices for all that
we have or do
light or dark
heat or cold
and all that's not truly us
we sever

Call it Truth or
simply Belief
something we've
bought that was sold
that rather than be a stone we're
a believer

But our days have been
burnished to greater shine
opening after opening
fold after fold

And of what we could not
do before
we deliver


4/17/2013, *The Soul's Home*

# APPLE PEEL EPIPHANY

I was peeling an apple in the sink round and round listening to a tape
  repeating the Name of God
When suddenly the peel went on forever extending past time and space
  as if ignited by the flame of God


Past walls and windows – out in the sky – past our planetary horizon
  completely –
The apple peel stretched way past even my own existence it seemed
  into the frame of God


It was only a moment – I don't mean to say it lasted as long as it seemed
But the peel went on spiraling under my knife as if in a whimsical
  game of God


Dizzy and bewildered for a second or two – holding the end of a mystical
  thread –
The peel uncoilingly reached into a mysterious dimension to the eternal
  acclaim of God


Mortal body in a material world – *Ameen* – things aren't at all what they
  seem –
Remembering God's true extra-spatial dimension seems to be a delightful
  aim of God!


6/7/2002, *The Flame of Transformation Turns to Light*

## SOME SHAFT OF LIGHT

We are all running in place in a
    shaft of God's Light.

I was inspired to this seeing a
young man running at 7A.M. wintry morning
    along the Schuylkill River in
        sweatpants and sweatshirt
flopping his arms, his face so innocent and
open, his mouth slightly open, eyes focused
straight ahead, running forward I guess as I
drove by, and it struck me we're actually

running in place in that shaft, sometimes
elevated, sometimes lifted out of ourselves, some even
raised to permanent levels, in

a shaft of God's perfect Light, not actually
going anywhere, not really
arriving from anywhere, our whole bodies

shaken up and down as if by the
force of our heartbeats, earth-shaken, quaking
mightily in place, faces as
innocent as birds, open to whatever
comes, mouths slightly
open as if to taste something sweet or say words,

some of us becoming suddenly
totally still, lifted
totally out of ourselves and replaced
entirely by God's
Light, that

same exact shaft we formerly were
running in place in, now

expanded from deep
within to way
past us, encompassing things that are
way beyond us,
eyes above seeing level, seeing
sights only few see, then
seeing straight into those who
face us, the
saintly ones whose sight's become
pure meaning,

while we continue to run in place in that single
shaft of God's Light,

fully alive in that running and

fully alive in that Light.


2/1/1999, *Some*

## HIS AUDIBLE SILENCE

God from First to Last is always the same.
Volcanoes erupt, tidal waves flash, cities disappear.
Each thing that happens is an appearance of His Name
rotating into action in this visible sphere.

This room in its post-dawn quiet surrounding here,
of the day's majestic light that spreads its glow
on common things that bob up to the surface to appear
then fade away like patches of late snow,

my pile of books, our life with its undertow
of time that drags it back while surging on ahead,
does not in any way affect, with all its crashing flow,
God, Who's Lord of all the living and the dead.

No thing that's added adds to Him a thing.
He in His audible silence makes all life sing.


6/1/1986, 22 Ramadan (after dawn), *Ramadan Sonnets*

# WE HAVE COME HERE

We have come here to be
where He is

Hello to distance
*Be in our hearts!*

Hello to the winds of where we
are

Take us to Him Who is where we
are

Tell Him we are here to be
where He is which is where
we are

If there was anywhere where
He wasn't there would be
nowhere where He is

But that is not possible
so He is Here


November 2013, #20, *He Comes Running*

# FROM THE SOFT ROPE WE ARE

From the soft rope we are
from the jagged tear in a canvas we are

from the wrecked and twisted bicycle we are
from the lengthy shadow of a lost world we are

from flickers at the edge of a dark wood we are
from an echoing empty stadium at midnight we are

from crumbs left for birds on a windowsill we are
from the signal sent from a ship's fo'c'sle we are

From land sighted and land ignored we are
from polished silver laid out perfectly we are

From a peak wreathed in roseate cloud we are
from a low-lying hamlet under brown smoke we are

From rows of burgeoning grape-trellises we are
from a sunny valley between green hills we are

From the spontaneous defenses of our sovereignty we are
from silence in the midst of chaos we are

From dust flakes falling down an endless chute we are
from an abrupt announcement at the table we are

From a door slammed and a door left open we are
From blue fog suddenly filling a deep canyon we are

From no one left in the meeting hall but us we are
from just one more face in the billowing crowd we are

From oft-blessed in abundance from we know not where we are
from bereft never knowingly visited by angels we are

From fervent supplications each dawn religiously we are
from the last whispered breath of prayer when we die we are

when even stillness stands still
right where we are

O God in Your Magnificence and Glory
Who moves us and moves in us

without Whom we would not be
whoever and wherever we are

Bring out from us what light You will
and quench us with every breath

in Your only existence
when no more than a shadow of a shadow of a shadow we are

Small flickering light in Your window we are
tiny birdsong of distant jubilant whistling

heard near and far
we are


9/5/2013, *The Soul's Home*

# Mysteries of Time

# ICE-SWANS

*for Malika*

The future's as bright as the
  eye that beholds it. The

past's as dark as the eye that
  shuts down its revisionist lids over what was,
in all its
  fluted subterfuges. Now the

present's another matter altogether. We're always going
on and on about the present, *the*
  *present this, the present that, be*
    *totally in the*
*present, the*
  *now is*
    *all there is*, whereas in fact the

present doesn't exist. As
  soon as it's
    passed our
      lips, it's past. We are a

momentary opacity before
  eternity's transparency. So much light getting
through sculpts us like a
    chef sculpts ice-swans just before the

banquet, but as soon as a
  form has fully emerged, or even a
little bit before, it starts
  to melt. When the

evening's over, a cold
    puddle's all that
      remains.
Forms disintegrate at the
peak of their perfection. Elderly

  couples waltz and
    fox-trot around it, beads of
      icy sweat roll down
    rounded wings, the
     fox-trotters also
       fluttering insubstantially before the

greater movement of the
    stars. A

larger dimension always
  engulfs us. No

need to cry out. The

demons have all
turned to butterflies. See, there they

go above the blazing farmhouse. Twilight catches

the falling
powder of their
wings.


4/14/1990, *A Maddening Disregard for the Passage of Time*

# TRAIN WRECK REVERSED

Time and space backtrack from the train wreck,
cars magnificently uncrumple, a deafening roar sucks
    back into the balmy silence of
      gnats and bird chirps in the
          precise moment preceding it,
a little black girl flies backwards through the air and
lands happily singing to herself
    by the side of the tracks,
people fly back unbloodying themselves,
lacerations smooth over and
torn limbs join torsos and return to normal,

some of the passengers
come remarkably back to life in the
    midst of an animated conversation, passenger cars
flip back onto tracks and are
coupled in their proper order, babies slip
miraculously back into cuddling arms,
passengers slip noisily back into their seats
    through the jagged metallic
      rip that closes now with the
      reversed sound of its ripping,
passengers pop back behind books, adjust
glasses, pick noses or
curl sideways on their seats with their
heads resting on greasy backpacks,

the horror on the engineer's face returns to the placid
concentration he's had for exactly
  an hour and twelve minutes, he
    sips his coffee and glances sideways at a
gauge,

gigantic bursts of flame go
back into the pinpoints of their sources like
genies zooming back into metallic bottles and
    pulling their corks in behind them,
angels surround the moving train
in their usual harmonious order, spectacular with
thought and gorgeous with
molecular obedience, moving through the air like
        raindrops falling from a cloud,

the critical moment hasn't come, history hasn't been
transformed, the flash of news remains
hidden in the future, newspaper reporters'
ears have yet to be bombarded with descriptions of
        disaster,
God's pre-eternal decree hasn't yet
revealed itself through the mysterious dimensions of
our bodies,

the nine-fifteen chugs along in the nimbus of
    its usual sense of
immortality, past pine trees and

farm houses,
accelerating slightly
as it heaves round the unforeseeable
        bend.


8/21/1995, *A Hundred Little 3D Pictures*

# THE ROWERS

The rowers of the big boats
had no letup

The trapeze artist has to
catch his mate

for once in midair it's
too late to be

elsewhere

A mortal born must go on
until there's no more

going on

then continues by his
Fashioner in His fashion

to where his Fashioner has
fashioned

Those explorers who went to the
ends of the earth and

perished in their tents

their own bodies their last frail
physical refuge

as the sleet continued to fall
the final resounding chord on the

planet's piano played

Alone in our beds
the brush against the

cheek of that nearness
having been born into

physical being it's
too late to be elsewhere

Having nothing at all to do with the
body is the saint's way

of astounding conviction
and God's direct Light

falling upon them
head to toe

inside and out

Looking over the edge of things
can we see any other way out?

But row the big boat
catch wrists in

midair
be peaceful in our

icy tents

bodiless Allah
our sole refuge?


6/4/2012, *Down at the Deep End*

# Singing & Dancing

*dedicated to Abdal-Lateef Whiteman*

# SINGING

*to my wife on our 17<sup>th</sup> wedding anniversary*

1

Over the distant marsh, across reed beds
  where geese are nesting,
    you can hear singing.

Out the downtrodden neighborhood window,
  across the rotted wooden window frame,
you can hear singing.

From between the loud metallic steaming
  railroad trains in the railroad station,
    in an overcast
gunmetal gray afternoon, clouds on
top of each other, you can hear singing.

From the house in the middle of a field,
grass peaked roof, cows meandering down a
  bright green hillside,
    you can hear singing...

At the end of a long road, Himalayan
  shadows where vultures circle
looking for a dead meal,
  you can hear singing.

Out at sea, from a sudden rowboat
  caught between troughs of water,
in the literal middle of nowhere,
  you can hear someone

    singing a poignant
wordless melody
to no one in particular...

and the crooner in the white spotlight
aboard a luxury steamer, late at
night, most people drunk, but
as he takes the microphone in the
full moon far out from any shore
suddenly everyone's sober and suddenly
   thoughtful about their mortality
and look across at each other
as the has-been crooner starts singing...

and this late night song of mine as almost everyone's
asleep, it's two-thirty in the
ante meridiem morning, my mouth is
shut, there's absolute
   silence except this
    world in words that's
opened up to my
     inner singing,

but the song opens out, it gets
louder and louder as the good earth turns in the
night and somewhere people wake up,
songs in their heads, get up to
   wash faces and shave and

notice they're singing, get as
naked as the day they were
born into a shower and put on the water
   full blast and find they're
belting out a song, and it

builds in momentum and sound, it
lights up the sky, the
    simple, exorbitantly
        gorgeous
sound of divinely inspired
(as everything else is!)

    singing.

2

The song is a blurt, a bleep, a
    song in a ditch,
a fly, a fuzz of fur in the
    air, a glint of light,
it's airborne, underwater, earthbound,
    over the top,
lighter than air, longer than air,
    a simple air,
air in the lungs, light in the lungs
    laughter, it's
clink of glasses, clunk of marble tabletops
    touching, clank of the
prison door,
    Clark Kent changing, that's it, it's
caterpillars pulling out their
    extended wings and
flying, youth turning into age
    and still managing to sing,
youth turning back into youth and
    singing, it's a
plane taking off, a blimp landing, a
    bicycle going down a hill,
wind in the hair, skating down a hill,

water current pulling,
undertow, tip-toe, do-si-do,
all of these and none,
the song is everything and
nothing
sung by God,
we live and die along its
rise and fall,
melody rising, melody falling,
    the song is alone,
the notes are dots of light in the
    endless night.
Night-night, night-owl, turn out the
    night-light.
Song of light lit like another
    star in the night.
Echo of song a galaxy sings
out in the night.

We sing the song for a while
and then we are light.


3/7/1996, *The Blind Beekeeper* (abridged)

# ECSTATIC DANCING

After an hour and a half of ecstatic dancing

After fifteen minutes of ecstatic dancing

After twenty-five-and-a-half minutes of ecstatic dancing

After just ten minutes of ecstatic dancing

After being held for just one minute to the central cyclotron of
ecstatic dancing

After being run down by stampeding horses of ecstatic dancing and
clutching tight to their glistening manes

After disappearing for long periods of time in the ramshackle
shack flying apart in ecstatic dancing

After one solid minute under the waterfall of ecstatic dancing

After sighting land afar off under pink clouds and
green sunlight in the brilliant golden sky of ecstatic dancing

After concluding then deconcluding in the
heightened inconclusive argument of the self shivered down to its
essential non-existence in the super reality of ecstatic dancing

After crickets and songbirds and every howling animal on earth
join together in the untouched Paradise of ecstatic dancing

After dreaming and waking up and then waking up
in the dream of being awake forever in ecstatic dancing

After plucking the ripe fruit and digesting it completely in just one
delicious moment of ecstatic dancing

After being transformed from a butterfly into a
freight train and from a freight train into a
redwood forest and from a redwood forest into a
snowy mountain range of weeping willows in the
moonlight and from that snowy mountain range of weeping willows
into pure moonlight itself in ecstatic dancing

After one breath of Allah taken and received and given out into the
world again in just one unbated breath of ecstatic dancing

And after the endlessness of this poem that will
continue long after it's finished in the endlessly
energized eternity of ecstatic dancing

After ecstatic dancing is done and begun again
and we enter into its core as we
were at the first and will be at the last again deathless and
breathless in ecstatic dancing

After just one second of ecstatic dancing

After God's blessed message excites us again
to ecstatic dancing

12/3/2002, *Through Rose Colored Glasses*

Ramadan

## THE INEVITABLE

It's like practicing for death. No food or drink
during daylight hours no matter
    what, in the
  heat of summer or
      cold of winter,
and no way out of it but through
    sickness, pregnancy, menstruation, madness or travel.
So that

it's something that comes
inevitably each year, like it or not, whether or not
you've got a knack for it, and
      some do, and love to fast, and
        thrive on it, but
  I do not, yet

each year it makes its visit, and year after
  year it builds up to be a
      sweet thing,

which makes it like death, the way it's
always on the
horizon, and an
absolute obligation, which must be
why Muslims often die well. They've had a
lifetime of Ramadans tenderizing them
for The Inevitable. And The

Inevitable surely comes.


5/9/1986, 1 Ramadan, *Ramadan Sonnets*

## RAMADAN SUNS ITSELF

Ramadan suns itself by the dark of night
and takes no notice of

earthquake or flood

Ramadan begins walking toward us from the
furthest hilltop of the previous year

and arrives at our door with
baskets of golden fruit

Although Ramadan seems most at home in
lavish "oriental" settings of jeweled

ewers and plashing fountains
our faces can best be reflected in its

battered tin plates and small sheltered ponds

No one has ever disappeared into Ramadan
never to be seen again

or if they do they appear again at the
Festival in bright silvery clothes

handing out sweets wrapped in our
most personal names

Ramadan is the most patient among us
and endures our anxieties with

perfect poise
never turning its face away

If we knew the treasures of Ramadan we would
want the fast to take place every

day of the year

but the sparkling gold of its coins dissolves into
denominational numbers when

Ramadan ends

If Ramadan were a horse it would be
a herd of the finest thoroughbreds

and each of us would be assigned the one most
suited to our variable temperaments

Ramadan is an ocean that waits each year in a
dimension of space and when it

bursts onto shore it
inundates our souls having transformed our

slightest actions into flying doves

Ramadan ends the way it begins
silently and with the

deepest humility

leaving through the same front door
through which it came

When the Prophet tightens his belt for
Ramadan each of us feels it

some losing and some gaining
the weight of its privations

Love arrives in the disguise of Ramadan
and when it removes its mask we find

it's been with us all along
as familiar to us as

ourselves

but more than we were before
and less


8/21/11, 21 Ramadan, *Ramadan Is Burnished Sunlight*

## GOD'S GARDEN GATE

By day we side with the unfortunate,
those who have little, and it makes us live
in a stark landscape, our energy spent,
doing small things and we give

up small comforts, existing in the wide spaces
between stars in a geometry of light.
Grim during the day, color comes into our faces
when we enter the gentle Bacchanal of night.

Then creation's natural feast lets loose its floods,
which circulate in streams in the body's beds,
day's darker starkness enters brighter moods,
our hearts are open, brightness frees our heads.

There is a tightness in fasting that makes us wait
in daily patience at God's Garden Gate.


8/25/1986, 25 Ramadan, *Ramadan Sonnets*

## RAMADAN IS BURNISHED SUNLIGHT

Ramadan is burnished sunlight on the
cheek of the Beloved at the

first dawn of creation

first fruits burst on first green
branches in the first Garden

their ripening a whole
lunar month without being picked

till they burst with the
celestial pleasure of pure being

Ramadan hunkers down in the extreme
depths of heaven and earth

simultaneously

as deep in the earth as the sky
bound together with immaterial

coils in the
knot of our fleshly hunger

It's a luminous door down a long hall in a
yearly wall in space

past rooms of resplendent solitudes and
incantatory gatherings with a

vision at the end of a tall silver stag whose
antlers are flames lighting our

way to inconceivable pastures
where endless bounty abounds

A weighty touch from an emptiness that
strikes sparks in our hearts

a turning from one light to another
even brighter than ocular radiance

Lick the tongue of it with our tongues!

Clear the throat of it with our throats!

Surround the sight of it in a blind blizzard of
overpouringness into our

suddenly increased dimension
as we stand a bit shakily at His

window
praising His Name


8/10/11, 10 Ramadan, *Ramadan Is Burnished Sunlight*

## GASTRONOMICAL RIGMAROLE

Fresh crisp cantaloupe spooned from its skin,
tamari-soaked almonds and mahjoul dates,
hot Ceylon tea with honey mixed in,
golden delicious apples on plates,

mango, stringy, sweet fit for potentates,
tropical specialty served on our table,
strawberries, nestled each with their mates
red as sunsets, delicious as fable –

tastes more pungent than words are able
to say without calling up alien likenesses,
each one basically untranslatable
into anything but their own sweet essences.

Häagan-Dazs coffee ice cream in a bowl –
I could go on and on with this
    gastronomical rigmarole!


5/18/1986, 10 Ramadan (evening), *Ramadan Sonnets*

# FINAL SONNET

From moon to moon the months go floating by,
one set for pilgrimage, one for fasting.
Filmy pictures of our lives pass like a fly
buzzing out a window. Only Allah's True Face is lasting.

Once a month or minute goes it can't come back.
Memory calls up fuzzy pictures, but the taste is gone.
Water trickles through wide fingers, but hands don't lack,
in slipping moisture, the always present moment to fasten on.

The present moment, mountain high, moonlight clear,
rises through the valley clouds of circumstance.
All altitudes are possible, all cliffs as sheer
as glass, or scenery gorgeous as a glance

in passing at a picturesque scene, *quick flash!*
God's Face stays. Our moments turn to moonlit ash.

6/11/1986, 19 Shawwal, *Ramadan Sonnets*

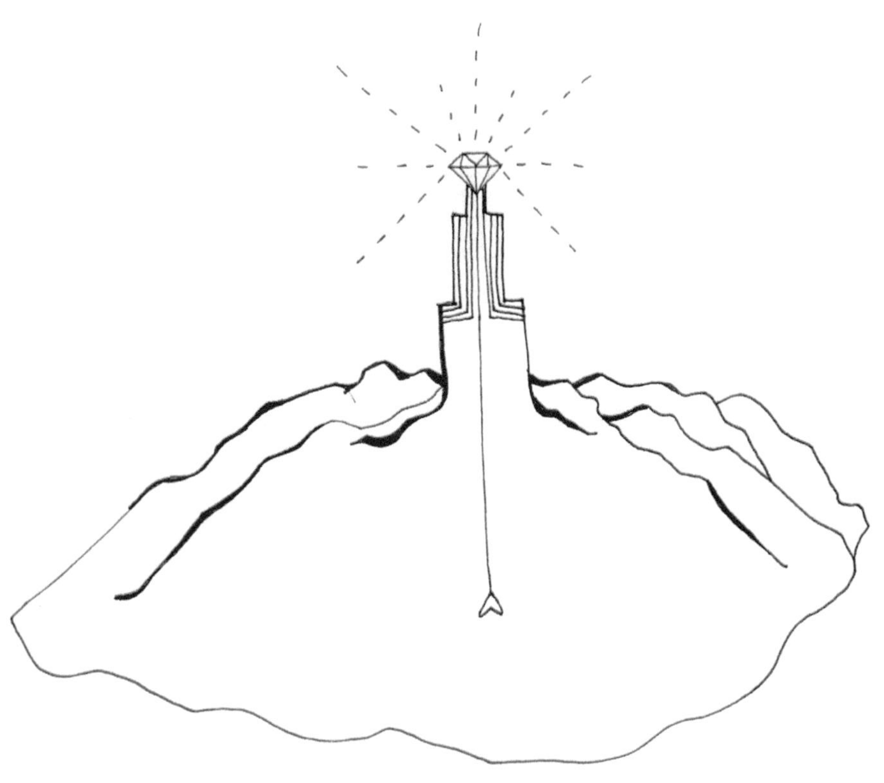

# Prophets & Saints

## ADAM'S INDELIBLE IMPRINT

And we're beaten on the ground of our
   own physical being
like someone taking the
   end of a plank and
   beating it on a rock,

we're beaten on the earth by our own
earthiness of being born, we're

beaten against the curved sides of
Father Noah's boat, against the
prison where beautiful
Joseph languished, against the
stake Abraham was tied to, against the
Kabah where the
blackened stone of light is kissed as we
swiftly pass by it to melt
back into the circling herd of
   similar hungry selves, beaten

like old clothes, washed in the
downstream and then
   stamped on by our

own feet which have
   Adam's indelible imprint. The

fast beats us with our own
   selves on the
     hard rock of
      physicality, it
takes us to the edge and makes us

look down,

it takes us to where there is
no escape and closes in, it

is the release of no release on a
day that does
end.

Even an eagle leaps into
no sure space,
hovers on an updraft
searching for food.

Hunger finally
ends. But so does
relief from
hunger.


5/10/1986, 2 Ramadan, *Ramadan Sonnets*

## ADAM STOOD IN THE WORLD

Adam stood in the world
as tall as the trees

the sun bathing his body
birds wreathing his outline with

birdsong
waters everywhere splashing

growls and grandeur of new animals
ache of new growths everywhere

sounding

Alone he stood with a
hunger in his heart reaching out to

touch the edible nothingness
around him

His own essence before his
birth in Allah's domain

nourished on Light and the Names he'll
name creation with

to keep each radiant thing linked to
Allah's single simultaneous

action in the unseen

each kind of leaf made consciousness
each cloud in passing also conscious

each Adam-named element
dimensionalizing the world

and the angels

all on prophet Adam's
fasting tongue

articulating even
now if we bend in

close to our hearts to hear
that original

soft sound


8/3/2011, 3 Ramadan, *Ramadan Is Burnished Sunlight*

# JESUS SAT ON A ROCK

Jesus sat on a rock amid the flames
and slowly and eloquently pronounced each name
of insect flower ditch cloud gate and harness
in order to release us from Adam's original
blessing which had become a curse
overlooking a thunderous ocean whose pounding waves
were also eloquent and whose watery syllables
also named both the great and small leaving absolutely
nothing out no nuance of psychic perturbation
moon-phase cloud-shape color of day or night and constellation

Finally Jesus arose and every water level on
earth rose with him every creature's body lifted slightly
and each being was re-infused with divine ringing
as in a cluster of harmonious chimes
running through their scales a million times in almost inaudible
tones so that we see that now every atom and every
atom's nucleus vibrates
from being called upon again by
Sublime Clarification's voice
setting it apart from mere chaotic noise


6/12/2001, *The Music Space*

## I SAW MARY BOARD A BUS AT BROAD AND STATE

*for Abdal-Hakim Murad*

I saw Mary board a bus at Broad and State
her head covered and her face radiant

small and held within herself
careful and preoccupied

a heaven seeming to be wrapped around her
her cheeks red her lips dry her eyes lowered

interior moisture her preferred cloister
the bus passengers sudden ghosts before her

her shoes small and tattered
her hands carrying a book

If any had spoken to her she might have become lost

If she had spoken to anyone
they might have become saved


6/9/2005, *Holiday from the Perfect Crime* (extract from the poem "Five Short
Meditations on the Virgin Mary")

# WITH THE SAINT AT THE WINDOW

The saint sat at the window and
became the window
that's what saints do

And the saint went out the window
and became the air
that's how they are

Animals feeding on the mountainside
saw the saint pass
they've got the eyes for it

The mountainside felt the saint pass
and her grasses bent aside
that's how saints go

On a saint's errand all things in place
for the remedy to arrive
on time as always

The twelve ducklings and the Chinese child
felt instantly renewed
though the saint barely touched them

Back before supper the saint wasn't missed
the place settings glimmered
as usual

Our earth is in need of them
our hearts are in need of them
God keep them at our side


3/31/2006, *Coattails of the Saint*

# IN RUMI'S TOMB AT KONYA

A sky shaped like a face – *no it can't be that*
A wingéd horse on fire in the middle of the air – *no it can't be that*

A sound of bells that burns from the feet to the heart
A whisper of hidden words falling from the top of the tree
    *– no it can't be that*

A look across the centuries that today is enshrouded in the world
The touch of a child's hand who already knows the secret – *no it can't be that*

A bridge of light in all the usual places
A bird that expands to embrace every living heart – *no it can't be that*

An eye that beholds the cave where the Prophet became Messenger
A sing-song voice speaking perfect rhyming sentences – *no it can't be that*

Hello before you arrive and Hello again before you get up to go
A kiss across green water that reflects both sun and moon
    *– no it can't be that*

A call from within Rumi's shirt so old its threads look like rain
A light that slides up a corner of the tomb and fills the body
    *– no it can't be that*

What is it then? Is there any answer?
Is it possible to say? – *no it can't be that*

*Ameen* was gone for a moment but something remained
There's only a trace left in the air from all of us – *no it can't be that*

Mevlana – we certainly had a magnificent celebration
Does it need to end? – *no – please – it can't be that*


5/7/2002, *The Flame of Transformation Turns to Light*

# WILL I STILL WANT TO READ THESE POEMS?

Will I still want to read these poems
if I have the chance

when the end comes?
Will they hold up to stark

reality's scrutiny? Or seem
trivial and beside the point?

Sick in Morocco
I woke up and saw our

hundred-and-one-year-old shaykh's benign face
hovering above me

touching my breast bone with his
divine hand and doing a

prayer for me

An hour later I woke up well may he be
blessed eternally

I can feel his touch on my
heartbone still

God's wind
blowing past my face

so sweetly

1/30/2014, *The Sweet Enigma of It All*

## AMONG THE GIANTS

*for Habib Ali and Habib Umar*

The lakes are quiet and the clouds are low
at the departure of all the giants from the world

Grasses bend in sadness and stones lament
in their lugubrious way because the

great ones have left us and now a silver night descends
and the seas are turbid and cold

Their broad smiles lit places where
even sunlight with all its atomic subtlety struggled to enter

Their buoyant hearts in every weather
reminded us of such a simple thing as our

pure humanity aloft in this earthly littleness and savagery

They walked among redwoods followed by equally giant sheep
they whistled melodious songs and birds fell from the

branches in a swoon

They brandished torches that lit up our frail battlements
and sad battlefields with a ruddy glow as if ready for an

early burning

Who remembers them except mountains in their
inaccessible crags and depthless gorges?

The clang of stones dislodged and hurtling into pits of
darkness?

Time itself measures their passing and space itself
feels the ache of such sudden shrinkage

Nights are longer than usual and
the small fires at the heart of them nearly

microscopic

Then one or two of God's saints appears and the
ancient brotherhood and sisterhood of the giants is revived

Highest mountain peaks capped in their otherworldly ice
recognize them as one of their own

Oceans sing from their netherwordly crevasses at their
arrival

Small of stature but filled with Muhammadan Light
their giant eyes and lengthy strides span

continents in one glance and oceans in one step forward

illuminating the arctic and undersides of the Northern Lights
as they shimmer their neon fuchsia curtains

with enough radiance for even the blind to
see by and get safely through to the end of the night


5/2/2006, *Coattails of the Saint*

# WAVING HELLO, WAVING GOODBYE

*A man came running from the far side of the city*
*Saying, "My people! Follow the Messengers!*
*Follow those who do not ask you for any wage*
*And who have received guidance."*
SURA YA SIN (19–21)

*In honor of Sufi Shaikh Muhammad Raheem Bawa Muhaiyaddeen*

There's a tiny speck on the horizon
We lean forward and see it's a human being
Coming closer closer ever closer
It's a man with a face like the luminous moon
He walks on a straight trail right up to our presence
He comes close and yet he's still far away
Is he waving hello or waving good-bye we'll never know
His light stains our garments like splashes from igneous lava
Like splatters of wax from the original Godly candle
There are vistas and landscapes that come along with him
Rivers of light that flow toward us with boats to take us
To a shore we've dreamed of but never clearly imagined
His face is not like most faces we pass on the street
His being is as luminous as the daylight as dark as the moon
There's something uncannily different about his atmosphere
When we get into its orbit something begins to happen
Even at the edge of the circle something takes place in our hearts
Some have seen him in person others have only heard of him
Some have even only heard of the ones who have heard of him
Yet in monotone singsong even they are illumined
For the speck we see on the horizon is so rare in this world.

He passed a few hours on the road with us swapping jokes and anecdotes
A little cosmic philosophy a few tall stories without final conclusion

A few wisps of spiritual gossip a few songs in monotone singsong as he passed
Reminding us in words of what is beyond human speech
Beseeching on our behalf what our own paltry souls barely know
He smiled in our direction but was it a smile of greeting or a smile of parting

We see a speck on the horizon
Is it coming toward us at last or going away?
Have we actually even for a moment understood what he was?
We jerk awake in the night with a sudden realization
We stand in his doorway where he passed to go into that light
His form and our form have actually melted into each other
Whether we recognize it or not we've been made over entirely
Our faces are not our own but our original face
Face that Allah created when He said: *"Be! And it is!"*

Like the ocean itself this story never ends so I'll let it go
And let the sound of the ocean itself continue it on
The speck on the far horizon never quite disappearing
The wave of the ocean itself never quite waving goodbye or hello
Ocean waves that wave both goodbye and hello forever
Waves in the sea rolling on and on in God's eye
Waving hello waving goodbye...


December 2001, *previously unpublished*

# Mawlid Poems

*In the Islamic poetic tradition, poems in praise of the Prophet Muhammad are assumed to include "Salallahu 'alayhi wa sallam," or "Peace and blessings be upon him."*

# MUHAMMAD'S BIRTH

About his birth the whole world knows
  in the depths of its atoms.

Amina bore him and he was immediate
  in his praise of Allah.

Some say he first did sajda, others
  that he spoke the shahada
    and then was silent.

Already at birth he was the Prophet of Unity, the
  movie played backwards
    from its glorious end.

His father Abdallah, from the tribe of Hashim,
  died without seeing him.

The wet nurse Halima took him to her heart
  and their goat's milk flowed.

All the desert burst into sumptuous flower
  from his singular presence.

The nighttime covered him
  with its spangled blanket.

The day fluffed the wool of its sides for him to
  tend it like huddled sheep.

A cloud went with him to shade him from the heat
  at the desert saint's surprise banquet.

(He could see the Prophet's space among the
    caravan leaders and
        called out for him to fill it –

*"Where is the boy who has come, by Allah,
    to show me the Prophet's seal?"* – a mole
  it is said, between his shoulder blades, with
        circling hairs like a horse's mane.)

He grew up trustworthy among men for whom
    this was a difficult quality.

He took from the cloth of Unity
the Black Stone of Eternity

and placed it bodily
in the side of God's House,

cornerstone finality,

stone we kiss

out of awe of God's Majesty.


1984, *Maulood* (published as part of *Sparrow on the Prophet's Tomb*)

# THE PERFECT MOON-FACED ONE

The perfect moon-faced one appears
with perfect lips and bow-like eyebrows.

His hair is braided behind his ears
and this pure appearance of his arouses

our trust that unity will thrive
and we'll be taken to One Presence

now that we find ourselves alive
in this world that is far less dense

than that of actions was before
when one thing made another happen –

here we find an open door
that there was only rarely open.

Praising, Praise, Praiseworthy, comes
hands raised at his sides, exalting,

takes us by our hearts and runs
through the various stations vaulting

past the barriers raised inside,
lusts and greed and deep reluctance,

knocks them with a touch aside,
keeps our steps firm with insistence,

leads us up no stairs to no height
but the one raised elevation

past the deepest realms of insight
to the Next World's happy station

face to face, our moon-faced one,
faces us past all formation,

praising that One with no space, sun
moon or stars, but all creation

gone in flashes no light shines on
to the last, uncluttered, single,

breath-stopped, stable, unique vision
in which all our gazes mingle

steady now, unchanging, direct
slow and slower eyesight finished,

just a mirror set to reflect
all the states, enlarged, diminished –

one breath streaming out past life
into worlds no eyes have seen.

There we find ourselves, no strife,
but one gaze that is evergreen

light upon a top-most tip
eye to eye, the "I" now gone –

emptiness, heart's deepest sip,
one gaze gazes on and on.

1981, *Chronicles of Akhira* (republished in 1984 in *Sparrow on the Prophet's Tomb*)

# KNOT OF GOLD

The Prophet took people of abject poverty
and strewed rubies at their feet

There was no glass in the Prophet's windows
for any brick to break

In each heart he ties a knot of gold
whose two ends make eternity's

radiant reclining figure eight
gazed upon by God

We can stand in the door he made in
our being or stride through it into God's

Presence

The Prophet never rode out on his she camel
but that they longed for his return


11/24/2007, *The Fire Eater's Lunchbreak*

# WHEN THE PROPHET CAME IN

We were sometimes noble sometimes venal
sometimes generous sometimes murderous

When the Prophet came in in his
usual way and sat down among us

His elegant brilliance never ceased to amaze us
and the fact that he knew what we
didn't know we needed to know

When the Prophet came in in his
usual way and sat down among us

We'd give up our lives for what he told us was true
while those of the rest of us kept
silent in his presence

When the Prophet came in in his
usual way and sat down among us

We might not have believed him
if not for the Qur'an which
made the material world immaterial and the
spiritual world real

When the Prophet came in in his
usual way and sat down among us

We who knew him before knew he was
telling the truth

when we saw the light that always went
with him

When the Prophet came in in his
usual way and sat down among us

The dust from his robes glittered like starlight
and his face in its brightness shone like the full moon

When the Prophet came in in his
usual way and sat down among us

And his resonant voice in its even
melodious tones had a jewel-like beauty
all of its own

When the Prophet came in in his
usual way and sat down among us

And if ever you were able to look in his eyes
and though he was shy he never
averted his gaze

When the Prophet came in in his
usual way and sat down among us

you might see Paradise in their dazzling light
as well as hear it in the words from his lips

When the Prophet came in in his
usual way and sat down among us

And we felt we were wrapped in wings of angels
and a few feet off the ground

When the Prophet came in in his
usual way and sat down among us

and every one of us felt suddenly wiser
listening intently to the depths of
what he was saying

When the Prophet came in in his
usual way and sat down among us

and all of us felt we partook of his beauty
his strength and purpose and above all
the Presence of God

When the Prophet came in in his
usual way and sat down among us

To sit in his presence was to sit in the Presence of
God all around and within us
now and forever

When the Prophet came in in his
usual way and sat down among us

and we took that realization with us
wherever we went and whenever we
remembered

how the Prophet came in in his
usual way and sat down among us

and to this day and to this moment I can
see him and feel his totally
humble but majestic presence

when the Prophet came in in his
usual way and sat down among us

It will never end till the end of time and
beyond time just as at the beginning
at the radiant creation's inception

when by Allah the Prophet came in in his
usual way and sat down among us

each and every one of us in
whatever state or station we
happen to be in

for the Prophet to come in in his
usual way and sit down among us

in spiritual presence and eternal
resonance glorifying that pivotal
moment in human history

when the Prophet Muhammad peace be upon him
came in in his usual way with no
pomp but in utter humanity

and sat down among us


3/11/2008, *The Fire Eater's Lunchbreak*

# BY OUR SMALLNESS WE KNOW YOUR VASTNESS

O Prophet of Allah, by our smallness we know your vastness,

by our electron microscopes we know in this world
how very little of the whole world we can know –

what shape we are in, what velocity through space, how
    organically we are connected
to everyone else in this race that has
   spread out so thoroughly from the
       loins of Adam.

Right now, our knowing ourselves to be alive,
that sense of total infusion between sound of
    motorcycle on the street outside
with the picture of silver-edged sublimity we have of you
superimposed in out-of-time dimensions
for the gesture of transmission to be triggered
1400 years ago through the tumult of time
      to now!

Transparency of leaf over leaf
in the leaf mold of totality!

Layered celluloid maneuvers of still pictures
    to the illusion of motion.

Has time elapsed since the first time
   Allah blew into His
     Light and said:

    *Be Muhammad?*

Has the fish embryo developed into rapacious shark
with slit eyes and merciless teeth
    who turns its white bulk
        and swims away?

The sands of Sayyedina Muhammad stretch in all
six directions at once!

Connecting us to that first sand grain
        puffed into space
that finds its place in the sea of a trillion grains
one so next to the other
or so on top of the other, or so underneath

in infinite array past
all mathematics but the supra-elemental
        accountancy
that goes on to a zero
that drops its silver egg
into the infinitesimal yawn of space
    who feels nothing
        and goes on as usual

since nothing at all has happened
but the repetition of the Divine Name
    on Its Own Lips

in the everywhere at once of original night.

O Prophet of Allah,
you were sent out of this

to tell us, being of it, to lead us, being
from it, to its

Source, its spark, its

original
one time

special
stopping place.


1984, *Sparrow on the Prophet's Tomb*

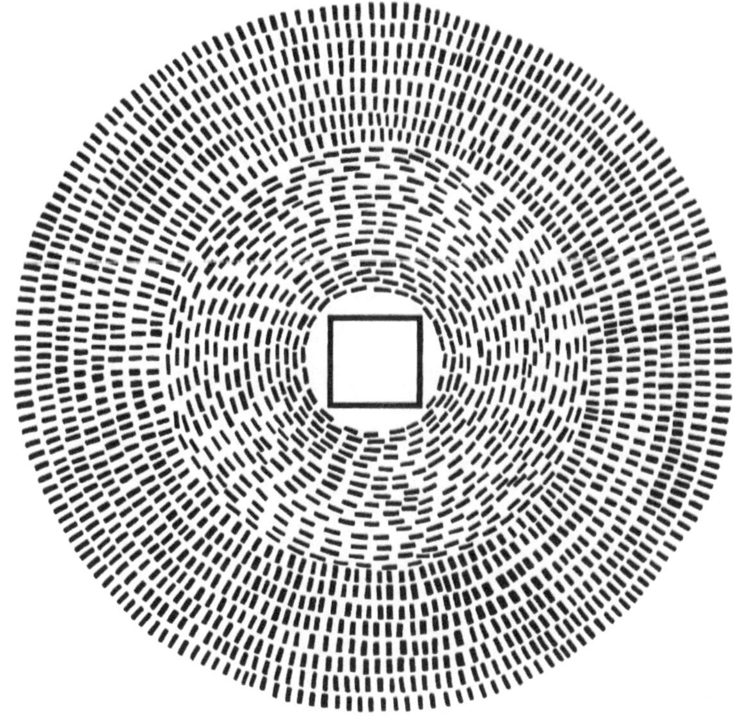

Pilgrimage

# WHO GOES ON HAJJ TO THE HOUSE OF ALLAH

Who goes on Hajj to the House of Allah?
Who takes the difficult journey?

Sets out from a house that falls into dust
and disappears as the front door closes

though to the family inside
its daily utensils have turned to shimmering crystal

its floor carpeted with
woven designs of cosmos and rebirth

Each step forward as we leave the world
is one step closer to God that encompasses miles

hovering ever closer to the House from which
flows every good and every light

centrifugally into our hearts

*

The roar of it
the surge of it

the circling of the square of it
the incomparable and inexpressible

awe of it

The indescribable out-of-proportion
of it

looming above the marble floor
the Kaaba's cubical black-shrouded silvery

glisten and the starkness of it
as we stand before it

suddenly bereft and lost alone in the cosmos
of it

held by it
held by the Lord of it

held to His House by the Majestic
Owner of it

now until endtime
and beyond

flooded by the
fluid solidity of it

Our bodies and souls exhausted by our
awe of it weeping in our

God-created beings
before it

Once seen by our own eyes
sighted or blind

never to leave it

Always from there
to have it central

far or near

Mecca His House and
God's Prophet's birthplace

nothing else like it
Nothing else

It
Itself

Alone
in The

total
Alone

of it


Date uncertain, *Facing Mecca*[5]

---

5    Abdal-Hayy came across this poem on his computer as he was editing *Facing Mecca* and couldn't remember writing it or when. He wrote: "Although not a part of the chronological series of *Facing Mecca*, stylistically written after 2000, it provides an appropriate coda."

# PRAYER AT THE KAʿBA

Oh Lord, the orange cat lying asleep on the
  shoe rack outside the Kaʿba
    looked tranquil, lean from
  living wild in Mecca, but still
    cat-like and sweet-faced –
surely some of this peacefulness
    could come to me?

Oh Lord, You raise up giant roof-beams in the
  world and
    hurl great foundations
      as deep as the seas –
I am only your creation of
    flesh and bone,
but surely some of those
    depths and heights
      could be mine?

Oh Allah, I sit here facing Your House on
  earth, beseeching Your Grace,
    seeking Your Face,
      my own not good enough in
        this life,
my own face a combination of
  lusty panther and
    awkward ostrich
  in this life,

yet I'm grateful for its
  miraculous properties in
    facing the world,

especially the eyes – close them
  and light spreads,
    open them and
      miracles appear –

especially Your stark square of black cloth rising
endlessly up into the night in front of me now
  but Your Face, Lord,
    could I catch a
    glimpse of it at least?

A white owl flies in the night somewhere,
its impassive face and saucer eyes
fleeing through the air.

*Is this my face, Lord,*
*searching everywhere?*


12/20/1995, *Mecca/Medina Timewarp* (published as part of *Sparrow on the Prophet's Tomb*)

# TWO SHORT POEMS

1

White moth on the
   black cloth of the Ka'ba
*Do you know where you are?*

2

I had a vision
everyone circumambulating the Ka'ba
turned into tiny white birds
   and flew away.


12/28/1995, *Mecca/Medina Timewarp* (published as part of *Sparrow on the Prophet's Tomb*)

# MIRACLE OF SOUND AT THE KA'BA

What sounds are heard around God's House?

First, utter silence, silence within silence. Then
        its echo,
    more silent still.

A silence that sits deep under the Throne of God –
all other silence surrounds it and
        slowly turns.

Every other silence partakes of that silence. Silence in
        eyes, silence in tongues, silence in the
womb, the silence of death.

The Ka'ba sits in the
shaft of that silence from the height of heaven,
and generates silence.

Then, just around this great circle of silence
the sound of an ocean, not of water or salt,
but of human longing, aswirl with
        sound, slow roar, slow-motion crash of
            surf, suspended animation of all
tremendous sounds in creation, the
exhalation of giant beasts, outbreath of
earth as God created caves and
        sea depths and

seismic shifts.

Then more distinctly,
articulating what shines through both

silence and sound,
the Word of God,
that aural text that floats from the
Heart of Light into the hearts of mankind,
tongue-tripped into articulate words, formed and
    filled with breath,
flowing like the sea, but from
    sea-depths of meaning,

light to the eyes and
sweet relief to the heart.

Then out from that circle,
the sound of all human speech, words of
    admonition, snatches of
        conversation, starlight of
God's Compassion sprinkled throughout it,
Turkish bursts, Arabic stutter, a child's distant cry,
then roar again, sea-surf,
silence,
silence above all, and the
    twelve-dimensional
        echo of that silence.
Then a phrase of Urdu, Afghani, Malay,
low rumble of
Qur'an recitation, pauses, people
    looking around, metallic
        clatter from far away, the
rhythmic supplications of a group of pilgrims
    circling God's House.

Then the click sound of a microphone in sonic superspace
    turning on.

Then words enveloped by the Word,

the Word enveloped in a roar,

the roar enveloped in silence,

the articulate silence of God, then

the silence of silence.

Then the echo of that silence.

Then the looking around.


12/26/1995, *Mecca/Medina Timewarp* (published as part of *Sparrow on the Prophet's Tomb*)

## SPARROW ON THE PROPHET'S TOMB

1

O sparrow perched on a corner of the
   Prophet's tomb
cheeping above thousands of bowed heads murmuring,
whose glassy chirps hit high notes of
   purity under the eaves in this
      Mosque of God's Messenger
that resides in two territories of space –
   this world seen, the next world
        unseen –

in this shadow existence of his signal presence among us
   visitors from even farther away than
      China pass by to greet him,
and in your little feathered body is the swooping freedom to
   come and go all day to visit him
speeding from a tall beam
   across choruses of hearts
gratefully weeping or tranquil with an ecstatic
      inner moon rise

just to be here.

2

Sparrow, what is your name? Is it *"Constant Devotion?"*
Is it *"I Want to Be Near?"* *"Praiseworthy Friend?"*
Is your name *"Generations to Come?"*
You fluff your breast and preen your wing
where men cannot go, you dart into the
dark of the tomb for deeper conversation.

We would all go with you if we could,
squeeze our tiny feathery bodies through the
    gold grille work, past the
        guards in their pea green uniforms,
to sit on a corner of the Prophet's tomb in the
    dark to hear him
return the salutations of
such outpouring awed adorations of men and women,
        each one
passing by that undying presence, trying to
sneak a peek through the golden porthole,
hearts boiling with overwhelming emotions.

You land and sing.
You cock your head.
You watch us from your high perch with a
    cool eye.

3

Sparrow, you are more than a sparrow.
You are a continent of sparrows.
You are The Minister of Internal Affairs of all
    sparrows.
You are the song that laces the margins of the deep message,
    the message of God's Magnificence, the
thunder of tremendous shock, earthquake and
    heaven crash of the
stark glare of God's Might.

You trill and fly,
your song like a tiny tune from paradise,
    delicate celesta of celestial light.

The mosque in Medina expands
  all the way to the
    ends of the earth.
Forget about walls, where
marble pillars mark
the mosque's original dimensions,
the Prophet's precincts now
    encompass our houses and the
  invisible courtyards of our
     love, interconnected by

sparrow-song, perched on a
  Turkish cornice,

singing to Timbuktu,
Medina song bird

  heard around the
    world.


12/26/1996, *Mecca/Medina Timewarp* (published as part of *Sparrow on the Prophet's Tomb*)

Prayer

# BEGINNING THE PRAYER

I stand facing Mecca
the house all around me
parallel with everything
hands up to my ears
   the Prayer begins

Hands across chest
   time-space capsule surrounds me
no god but Allah
   all Other forgotten

Here's eternity's signature
   signed through space
with severe strokes

Parallel lines on the prayer mat
   past actions cast behind me
     trees in linear groves
stand straight in the Prayer in
   this world
bend from the waist
    into the Next

There are parallel lines
   to the limits
past the
   edge of the
earth are darknesses
the body stands straight then
   prostrates
what does it bow to but
   Absence

Absence that is a
   Presence
we can't see with our bare
   eyes but know
eyes don't see Allah's Presence
      physically
but are themselves
      proof by
pure seeing

His Absence Alive in the air
we prostrate in parallel lines
we stand straight with
      angels in the prayer line
rows of Mediterranean Cypresses
   tall silhouettes against white sky
favorites of foggy graveyards

We stand with
   arms at our sides
against the
   beating chests of our
      turmoils
clasping left wrist with right hand
eyes half-slitted
   not staring

Gaze made to
   fall on the
inside
last actions done
   cast behind me

Dead while alive
standing still
    concentrated
by praying

From the
Next World we
rise into

This one


5/16/1989, *Facing Mecca*

## DAWN PRAYER

I stood before my Lord at dawn
  and for a moment I was a
    fiery tropical lily, orange with
      yellow spots, a blue sky
    in front of me,
I was a pane of glass with iridescent striations,
I was a symphony orchestra under water,
I became a long shadow cast in sand of a
   city in ruins or an
     oasis withered to stalks,
I was the expression on an old woman
    watching her last grown son leave home...

I stood before my Lord at dawn
on the lip-edge of creation
and I became a canyon space full of early
    fog, a panorama for clouds
      to pass in,
     shifting pastel shapes,

I prayed before God and
  became a dark river with early morning
    voices of men setting out in
      canoes – echoes, cries –

I became a space in which things happen,

I became a space where prayer happens.

3/6/1996, *Miracle Songs for the Millennium* (abridged)

# ON THE PRAYER MAT

On the prayer mat tonight facing Mecca I feel
  about to burst,
    atoms like those
round puff-pockets in packing padding kids love to pop
  but on a
    vast scale, spread throughout creation, trees, skies, hills, clouds, those
molecules of light stretched through everything that
  exists for a moment, and it
happens so intensely because my movements are so
    constrained in the Prayer, I can't just
get up and walk away, but must
stand, bow, prostrate, sit, while all the time I'm just about
to spray atomic being in all directions, or I feel the
Light of it smashing!


6/2/1989, *Facing Mecca* (extract)

## WHAT SWEETNESS IT IS

What sweetness it is, in a
  sea of bleakness, to
    prostrate in the
      prayer!

The Prophet, peace be upon him, said it was
the coolness of his eye.

Just about at the
  edge of endurance, not wanting to do
    much of anything, but having one
more prayer to do before
  sunset, I stood, my
plum shirt glowing in accord with the
  plum color in the
    prayer mat, the
bird out of his cage, pacing back and
  forth on
    top, the sound of
water spray from the
kitchen somewhere in back of me, I

stood to do the
prayer, and an
immediate
sweetness
  came over me, and a

kneeling that was like the
invisible disappearing down into the
visible as I
prostrated before the

Invisible
  Presence

and felt
sane.


6/5/1986, 28 Ramadan (before sunset), *Ramadan Sonnets*

## DOOR

Dear Lord – five times a day we stop everything to face Your door –
Five times a day we try to draw close by turning to face Your door

We put the world behind us as our hands go down from our ears –
We stand straight on our own two feet in the place of Your door

Are You there behind it as it faces us – do You hear our pleas?
His Message assures us Your Presence really does grace Your door!

But what is it – this direction we face away from our selves and the world?
That only one thing remain as our selves begin to efface – *Your door!*

You're nowhere else – being everywhere and nowhere – as we disappear –
We stand the exact shape of ourselves in the divine space of Your door!

We stand and bow and prostrate until our hearts are above our heads –
Our hearts incessantly beating for reply – Truth's embrace – at Your door!

If the whole earth is a mosque for us – hills – valleys – plains –
      the living room floor –
Yet to stop and turn where there is nothing visible – ah! –nothing can
      replace Your door!

It's not of this world – it's Yours alone – Allah – the dimension of prayer
      heart to heart –
World falls away – we're suspended in space – it's a celestial staircase –
      *Your door!*

And in the prayer we say ameen and *"Peace be upon you!"* at the end –
And after the prayer we leave nothing behind – no physical trace – but
      Your door!

And as we approach – step by step – heartbeat by heartbeat – to adore –
We hope to catch at least a fleeting glimpse of Your resplendent Face –
        Your door!


5/27/2002, *The Flame of Transformation Turns to Light*

## THE BEAUTIFUL DU'A

My Lord, of Whom, O God, there is no god but You,
we are Your humble slaves like gathering bees on earth
and You are our Benevolent King in the gorgeous splendors of
Your universe,
in the great invisible Throne room of the starry heavens
and of all the leafy glades and hard roads of Your creation
over which You alone are sovereign,
and You have granted us a spatial door out of our daily lives
which is the ritual Prayer to You,
an open glassy corridor of light and space
away from the rough clash of arms and dazzling neon catastrophes
of our days,
and You are the only One to Whom we can come to ask,
our hearts can sail like flying fish into Your loving space through
the door of Your Prayer in open song
with their deepest pains and profoundest yearnings,
we are weak and You are strong,
we are wild and You tame us,
we are in need always
and You are the Giver of Your Bounty with every breath,
All-Knower, knowing us better than we know ourselves,
Opener to what is always openly best for us,
Guiding us away from what harms us
even as we wish its forbidden succulence for ourselves,
O Allah, Merciful and Compassionate,
let us see Your Face on each horizon and in ourselves,
make us always pleasing in Your sight,
bless those dearest to us as well as those far away who need
Your blessings most,
You are our God Alone to Whom we turn, away from the world,
we throw ourselves with complete confidence
through the open space of your Mercy and Generous Love,

and look to Your Prophet for
Your guidance among humankind,
and blessings on him and his blessed Family and Companions
as many as there are atoms spinning in this universe of Yours,
as many as the tiniest ripples on sunlit seas and in the darkest deeps,
as many as glints of light that illuminate our days
and fill our hearts at night,
until the end of time. *Amen.*


Date uncertain, *previously unpublished*

*Ecstatic Love*

# LOVE

Love is a nectar pressed from a
     silvery grape
          plucked from the Unseen
     just hanging ever so slightly
          over the Garden wall into

this world. The vine has
many delicious souls incorporated into its
     maze. The arbor is the place for
          bells. Each touch of wisdom's
wind matures the grapes, and their
fermentation is love.

We cannot talk about love in the street-digger's ditch.
We can't talk about it
     hip-deep in mud, with the
          stink of the
world on our clothes.
Then it is only the loud
     laughter of
          quick relief, not the

arduous journey.

We have to talk about love in the
place where the
     pure drunks congregate who know the
          bell-clear Name of the
               Beloved, and are
     not afraid. It is a
place of proclamations, and
lack of all restraint. It is a

place where the next world's boughs hang
   close to the earth within
      easy reach.

Slender herons fly across the silhouette of love's foliage
   at angles in a white sky.
Love is a scent that has
the gaunt-eyed standing at
   newly opened doors
      begging for
         audience.
Love weaves hair into Renaissance knots
   with tiny neon flowers
only the wisest bees
   discover to sip its nectar.
Love is a terrible wave only the
   most intrepid navigator
dares enter. Let us not
talk about love. It
cannot be mentioned in the
   marketplace. In the
boardrooms of America
   love has gone astray, and the
      object misplaced.
Love is a harsh master
jealous of duplicity. Love is a

lone eagle proud on a harsh rock.
Love is a faint glow in the distance on the
   high seas, but
      enough for the
   lone survivor. It is the

pocket of calm between two
rough sheets of sandstorm.

It is the
sandstorm itself.

It is a taste that will test the taster
who gives up all doubts and takes a
    leap that leaves a chasm
        forever between what he
once was and what he has
    now become. Time turns the
gulf into a canyon so wide
        there is
        no turning back. Love is a

mysterious guide on a mist-filled mountain path
that winds around severe peaks, and
    passes caves cut into the
liquid rock-crystal of dream. But it

goes past them.

There is no animal capable, in all its
    animal innocence, of
        embodying the
    full dimension of love.
Love is not for
the lower beasts, even though their
    loyalty partakes of a
        portion of its sea.

No space of creation is without it. Even in the
darkest depths of the sea.

It drives us on.

It takes hold.

It brings some into the
land of a foolishness so
   wise only
few understand its
    language. Birds
understand it. They stitch the

daylight skies with its
syllables.

The brilliant
   light of silence
knows it.

The hopeless lover with

moist eyes

knows it.


5/31/1986, 23 Ramadan (morning), *Ramadan Sonnets*

# THE DRUNK IN ALLAH

The drunk in Allah are
free from the roll of the dice

The drunk in Allah swim in the
mercy of His love

The drunk in Allah take both
roads at the fork

*(and do so because they're
drunk in Allah)*

The drunk in Allah eat caviar when they
eat dry biscuits

drink the best vintage wine when they
sip water

They're here hobnobbing with ants and
butterflies and converse at length with

the spider in her web

The drunk in Allah would never let on
they're drunk in Allah unless they're

drunk in Allah

They enter a hospital and come out
shaking like an invalid

enter an old people's home and come out
the death of all of them

enter an orchestra and come out the
whistle on a garbage barge heading into

gray waters

The drunk in Allah have
one thing in mind put there

by Allah

Having given up themselves they're
brought into sunlight like

washing set out to dry

They don't do anything on their
own anymore

If a bricklayer hired them the
wall would be done in a flash

or it might take a year
or never

Drunk in Allah


5/3/2010, *In Constant Incandescence*

# I'M IN LOVE WITH A PANTHER

1

I'm in love with a panther. I'm in
love with her claws, with her
savage breath and those teeth on the
  cutting edge of danger. I'm in

love with her eyes which see in a way I
can't know, not with
human seeing, green-gray, they

flash in the night, spotlit, as if the
light comes from deep inside her and is
laser beamed through her pupils outward. I

love her sleekness. She can be ahead of me in
a pounce, her back flanks rippling with
sheer power. Terror

in the air as she leaps forward. I love that she's
distant from me in nature, I'm bound by her
strength over me, she could
kill me in a wink and

probably will, most certainly will, when I
least expect it, from the side, or from in
front, with sweet and
ample preparation, closing in on me gradually,

I love that, I love her darkness, sheen of
burnished velvet, she is erotically
charged but far beyond such

passing passions, she

flattens next to me and flicks her ears. She's picking up
faraway sounds. No sound
     escapes her. I love the

shadow she pulls close across me, starting from my
toes and moving upward to my
scalp with hair standing on end.
She looks me full in the eyes, but when I
     gaze into those eyes like
          freefalling on a night of
absolute blackness, falling deep
     into them, it's nothing

familiar, nothing I can easily translate, it's
     cuneiform hieroglyphics and the
calligraphy of an enticing death, that we

both get wrapped in a black fur cloak and that we
lose our distinct identities, and when the
smoke clears we're at ease among her
rocks at her accustomed height, just
     above the tree line, noses

pressed against a sky so pristine white
it's like the inside of shell.

2

Her teasing only makes me ask for more.
Reality goes way past metaphor.

She takes me to the edge and I look down.

She crouches forward, face impassive, yawns.

Miles down the rock face is her element.
She's part of shale and schist, rock, cement.

As easily as down an office building's slope
I look down with my panther at my side, hopeless

as well as full of hope. Black thing. Gorgeous
as death is. Through valley gorges,

peaks, stealthily as well as obviously she goes.
Her blackness starkly silhouetted when it snows.

I'm dandled, played with, left alone, surrounded.
Everywhere I go I'm panther-bounded.

Her purr's a sound like no sound ever sounded.
Her growl like gurgling tree roots, primordial groan.

With her I'm never lonely, yet alone.
Her roar puts out the night, lights up the moon.

3

My panther who blends into the night
and is gone. Present but

not plainly visible.
Her formlessness spreads out across the sky at dawn.

*6/24/1998, Salt Prayers*

## CREEDS

If divorce is the only way divorce with civility

If despair is the only way despair with dignity

If fear is the only way fear with humility

If censure is the only way censure with humanity

If judgment is the only way judge with temerity

If desire is the only way desire with frugality

If ambition is the only way be ambitious with integrity

If reason is the only way reason with spontaneity

If love is the only way love with totality

If travel is the only way travel with variety

If submission is the only way submit with alacrity

If love of God is the only way love God with consistency

If arrival is the only way arrive with ecstasy


9/27/2003, *Love Is a Letter Burning in a High Wind*

# THE MOTOR RUNNING

Three drops from the ocean of love fell on the
hem of my shirt
though I could hear its crashing surf far above both the
stars and the liquid daylight
and it crashed on the earth like hands slapping
dough to be made into bread
or like a whisper in a room so silent
everyone can hear

Three drops alone reached me but I'm now
helplessly drunk since the sender of these
drops though coquettish is made real by the
moisture and shape of the drops
one drop for loyalty one drop for eternity and the
last one for death whose car door is always
open and the motor running


4/7/2002, *Where Death Goes*

## THIS IS THE MARRIAGE

*for my daughter Salihah*

This is the marriage of a
very small horse and a giant green valley
at the dawn of the world

This is the marriage of sea foam and the
wind that blows it into spray

This is the marriage of a dark cupboard and a
hand that reaches in looking for diamonds

This is the marriage of all our faces to the
soul that makes them smile then makes them weep
then makes them smile again
a turquoise songbird and the emerald
branch it lands on

This is the marriage of sky and stars
light extending by day but going out by night with
a million lanterns to see itself by
self-illumined, eyes ablaze, singing at the top of lungs
like our hearts

This is the marriage God wanted with us
before the creation of the world
before the Gate of mist and topaz opened
before the gorgeous fires around the edges of things ignited
alive squiggles outlining each loveable entity

This is the marriage of two people in a canyon of glass
under a real sun in a

procession of elephants and gazelle
both bringing the entire biological mystery together
to be delicately tied tendril by tendril into the knot of life
watched over by eagles wheeling in the sky
by blind worms deep in their earthly meditations

This is the marriage of a
room and going into it
of a house and entering by the front door
of a country and obtaining a valid passport
of the air and the mockingbird's song that flows into it
of a river and setting out in a green canoe to explore
new continents and their whispering people
and the extraordinary black orchids that grow there in the dark
in even the worst of circumstances

I call on the colors of the rainbow to bear witness
    sun glint on wave troughs

I call on the very thoughts that pass through our heads
at this instant to bear witness

O God, we are your loving creatures
still dew-sprinkled from the first
    deep ache of creation
trying to stand full height in a strong
wind to call on You

Fill their youth with the wisdom of the seas
God's navigation by the stars
the sound of waves calling His Ninety-Nine Names
one by one and all together, never asleep

This is the marriage of our feet and the very

earth they stand on

The bodies we stand in
sinew by sinew and the inclinations of our souls

Two bodies a man and a woman
gazing at each other from their
facing towers of parakeets and milk pitchers
nasturtiums and spontaneous song
desire for perfection and deep knowledge of God in the heart

And we bear witness to it
before foam passes over a waterfall
and is gone

Before the flower of our lives becomes married to the
root of our deaths

With a tiny white horse in a green valley
at the dawn of the world

And we ride away into the light


6/15/1999, *I Imagine a Lion*

*Family*

## O MY LOVE

O my love needs not to be split
   between the Origin and Cause of things
   and my wife with sudden softness
     and sure heart,
for her beauty as she moves
is none other than the
      Origin and Cause of things
        directly manifest.
Her light from eyes and shining intellect,
her words which coil with mine to make a
      swirling rope of light is
       His, the only eloquent One
       in all the worlds.
To see her is to be reminded
     Face of her face, Light of her light,
      swiftness and grace and hidden majesty
of her noble impact on the air itself
   as she moves through it
    to meet me halfway
between this world and the next.

When our eyes meet and we both look deeper inside
it is the act of the Origin and Cause of things
Who has made such sensate pools resonate
in this world of His,
    they reverberate off time and space, they
light up hidden crevices and cool lagoons
    under the mossy ledges of the ancient ones,
the oldest loves and their glory, the oldest
    cares and their careworn final
     sighs of ultimate submission

exhausted when the last breath
    slides out to go to the
Origin and Cause of things at last
    to lay down its arms
and see the pure love of which all these loves
      were partial,
the whole gem of light of which all these loves
      were facets,
to see the unmistakable Unity behind the
glamorous technicolor sights that so
    blasted our hearts and eyes
      filling them with the multiple
    details of indivisible delight.


1984, *The Desert Is the Only Way Out* (extract)

# OF MY MOTHER, 92, WITH ALZHEIMER'S

1

I hate to think she may no longer dream of me.

She lies on her couch and stares at the ceiling
   like a bird. Blinks and keeps
staring. Her arthritic fingers like bird claws.
But her face also reminds me of a cat's,
looking completely with seemingly unseeing
      eyes. Then comprehending. Then
not comprehending. Her

frail, cold form, cheeks sunken, hair so usually
carefully kempt, now spreading out white and
lank and long behind her head on the
pillow, hair I'd never seen not in some
beauty shop cut, now left to
   nature, oblivious to fashion. Ancient.
Crone hair. Mother, my dear affectionate
mother, a crone. But a

sweet crone. *"Should I be here? Is this
where I'm supposed to be?"*

Blinks. Recognizes. Loses the
   thread.
There on her perch in a kind of
   silvery nowhere. Who
took me downtown to the movies, by bus, later by
car, who dressed me warmly, snapping the
   leather strap of my
      cap under my chin, who

took me across the Bay Bridge to
San Francisco on the train (the span under the
automobile level above), and I

remember so pungently the smell of the
Hills Brothers Coffee factory on the
San Francisco side, and the
  coffee cup up-tilted ecstatic
Arab in yellow robe and white turban bigger than
life on the billboard. That was my

mother who took me there, who tilted her
head and smiled, and flirted, and hated her
round gray mother for flirting, and she even

now flirts on the bed, face up at me, winking,

frowning, opening eyes wide, pulling down her
mouth, then smiling that heartbreaking

mother's smile. My

mother's smile.

2

The Prophet Muhammad said Paradise lies at the
  feet of mothers, and I
know it's true.
My mother lies there with
Paradise at her feet, frail feet now in
soft moccasins, barely able to get her to the
bathroom with her aluminum walker for support,
her thin blue-scribbled legs, whiter than paper,

yet Paradise is there. She

spoon-fed me. That's the
fountains of Paradise. She
held me close, that's the
affection of Paradise, and worried herself to
death about me, and had the
dread despair, and was so

glad when I called, and looked into my
face now long and hard and
put her arms around my
neck with extraordinary almost vicelike
grip to kiss me, and though her

kiss, so dry, so cold, lips weathered, was
the kiss of death, on me and on her, it was the
kiss of life, a mother's kiss, which is the

endlessly flowing rivers of Paradise with a
supernatural light flickering along their ripples,

and the air of Paradise is the mother's atmosphere,
where she walks, where she

lies stretched out now, hands plucking a
coverlet, veiled eyes fastened on the
ceiling, already more in

Paradise than here. O God, may You

take her there!

3

Silver-haired Siberian mothers!

*Hoolah!*

Stalking snow-deer, a bone clenched between their teeth,
silver eyes clenched against
    storm, determined to get there!

*Hoobah!*

Natural Wisconsin mothers on cow farms in denim
    skirts and boots of rough leather, rope
burns on hands, faces of raw cow milk,
cheeks of burnt straw, eyes of hot
        water!

*Ooyah!*

Moccasin mothers against high winds putting
feather skin capes over moon-faced papooses,
cowering in teepee dark, hearts beating deep,

*Cachaw!*

Mothers in circle making quilt, toothless,
    once-beautiful, lissome,
nimble-fingered, breasts bone, breasts now
    dry as bone,
lonesome in their plenitude,

*Bashah!*

Mothers and more mothers, floating horizontal, head to
toe, great rings of them revolving
    around the globe!

*Hooshah!*

Mothers everywhere!

Living in wood crates on Chinese docks,
palaces with carpets five inches thick,
    high rises, tenements,
the projects, the dumps, scrounging supermarket
    tips, dipping croissants in
thick cream in outdoor Parisian cafés to feed their
young, birds in the air, mouse mothers in
holes, my mother in
California waiting patiently for death.

*"Should I be here? Where
should I be? Is this all right? What
are you going to do now?"*

"I'm just going to sit with you for a while,
    Mom. I'm just going to
hang out with you for awhile."

*"OK."*


4/1/1998, *You Open a Door and It's a Starry Night*

## LEGACY

1

I wonder if a father looked deeply inside himself he'd find
what he really wanted for his son, or whether he'd find
as much bewilderment in the world for his son as he
finds for himself, surrounded by the
roaring iron lions of commerce, the
vivid dream-figures of
Quest, with all its cardiac pressures and
sudden, occasional divine clarities, but
the world like a domain of green prairie as far as
the naked eye can see from
one curved sky to another, and the
clouds in the son's life as
unreadable in their puffing masses as they are to
his father, now, on earth, among now's mortal crowd.

Would the high-wire aerialist envision his
son in white tights on a silver bicycle in
crossing spotlights at the same
hair-line between
daring and death, feeling
the same mastery, precision, thrill of
one more death-defying danger foiled?

The drum rolls.
The spotlight comes to rest.
A hush. The father is gray, his once firm muscles slack.

Throws off his cape and

out of his chest steps a son who stands on the
thin wire above the crowd perfectly poised, and
out of his chest steps his son with a sweeping bow, and

out of *his* chest steps his son who leaps in the air

and lands on the
wire on one hand.

2

*"Ah, I leave you such an imperfect world,"* says the
father who's missed the point.
Standing in the midst of it all but thinking he's
somehow the author of it, and that somehow he's unable to stop the
destructive drift of it.

A king in his throne room playing with
wind-up toys on his
ivory table for his son, while
just behind him is the
avalanche of One Eyed Dragon Mountain, and the
son in brocade has to
walk without royal robes through the
falling streams of that avalanche, seeing if he can
charm the rocky chunks to slow-motion,
charm the down-drag of gravity to
soften its pull and bring
this life into peaceful quiescence at last.

*Every man's task.*

3

The world as I found it,
brown nut in a loose bag,
reindeer on the tundra,
bright skies, wise skies,

knock your pipe on the washstand,
little door in a big house,

smooth rope hanging in a well,
bluejay on a clothesline,

desktop cluttered with books,
alchemist's knucklebones,

flash out the window, start the car,
staircase in a clockwise spiral,

mouse-noses twitching over breakfast,
enter the world a noisy guest,

leave the world a sober one,
while you're here sweep the floor,

while you're here listen to birdsong,
the world as I found it,

leave it alone,
wear it out

next to your skin,
the world as I found it,

brown nut in a loose bag,
the world as I found it,
my son and all sons after him.


7/4/1991, *Like When You Wave at a Train and the Train Hoots Back at You*

## MY DAUGHTER

*for Salihah*

My daughter sits very still on the
petal of a camelia on the
waters of a small shaded pond.

She is fifteen going on sixteen

shaped like a young Mongolian horse
with a flying mane and full flying tail.

Her heart is the scherzo of a particularly
    moving trio by Beethoven played on
        glass instruments.

The world is beckoning to her like the smoky
        post-midnight part of a
particularly honky-tonk port city with
    snaky neon signs and snare drums,
and her ears, like the new wet wings of
        tropical butterflies,
flutter slightly and appear about to
    detach themselves and fly in the
        direction of the sound, but
remain instead on the sides of her head
fanning slowly back and forth in the sunlight
        to dry.

Her heart is an entire forest of streams and
    underground water basins,
a very beautiful and serene primitive
    tribe lives on the banks of its

        rivers who have no word for
"hatred" or "warfare"...

Her heart is a long moonlit stairway in somewhere like
    Vienna, stone lions on pedestals
        protecting it.

It is a very beloved place to God, her heart,

a place of small pleasure boats and
echoing laughter over splashing water.

her heart is new and cries out, protects her
vulnerable friends and her friends'
    vulnerabilities and often forgets
        her own.

She is a very beautiful white mythical
    galloping animal on the
        rim of the ocean, small
hooves beating green foam.

My daughter is a grown girl and a
newly formed woman.

Her long dark hair belongs to the
natives of far Pacific Islands.
Her eyes belong to herself and see through
    long dark lashes
that easily fill with tears, my daughter,
my own flesh and blood, she is

a new continent over a dark
unexplored area of the globe,

but the music we already hear from the
villagers is naturally rhythmic

and played on sweet instruments.

My daughter is one of God's sweet instruments
playing slow scales in a shaft of
burnished sunlight, flute-like and bright,

trying out melodies in this life
never quite played before

but as ancient as rain.


3/12/1996, *The Blind Beekeeper* (abridged)

# I WANT TO TALK TO YOU

O.K. I want to talk to you in a way my own father
never talked to me. I can't remember
a single conversation we ever had. We
never talked about anything important. *Can you
believe it!* It's like
explorers taking off their clothes and running
stark naked into uncharted
territory with
no ammunition, no amulets, no articles of
trade – you've got to
make it all up from scratch when your own
male dad can't transmit anything of weight to you to
use! But all he had to do (not even

gray woolen monk's robes, astrolabes or arcane
scrolls) was just share a bit of
candor and reality, a few
simple exchanges on a park-bench, a nod of
understanding that meant something more than just
a male conspiracy against mom's
enveloping dimension.

Not that I've got that much to transmit to you
from masculine experience, neither
boat-building skills nor computer wizardry, all the way
down to a suave and cavalier ability to make a
living without expending
desperate energy, I haven't even got street-smarts
hustler mentality!

But still I can
hope to give you

some candor and reality, or at least try to make it
possible to find
some of it
together. A bit of

candor and reality.


6/12/1991, *Like When You Wave at a Train and the Train Hoots Back at You*

# Funny Poems

# EXPLANATORY NOTE

I've just had one of the most
      bizarre experiences of my life. Putting the
cap back onto my
         fountain pen at 3:00 a.m. just after
writing *"Flights of Angels,"* the cap fitting tightly, so
being sleepy, I was struggling a
         little against its
   tightness, the pen slipped and the
point went right into my left thumb, tip
puncturing thumb-pad, injecting me with
      ink. It
bled, I squeezed it, pulsing
   drops of blood mixed with tiny black streams, ran
thumb under faucet, put Neosporin on it, lay
   down on bed awaiting instant
      death, feeling my
         feet sort of
cramp up, imagining wildly that I might get
ink poisoning and die, the puncture now almost
invisible, then my
   wife would
   find me dead in the
      morning and
not know why.

Later, after autopsy: *"Poet Dies With
   Ink in His Veins."* Inkstream inside his
bloodstream writing
   fatal odes on the
      inner walls of his
         heart.

*(I left my notebook open to this poem by my bed, just in case)*

248

7/29/1991, *previously unpublished*

## NEWSPAPER FANTASY

I opened the newspaper this
morning and all the

type slid off onto my lap

I rearranged it to read:
*"Angels Sighted Over Major Cities"*

*When radios were turned on this*
*morning all that was heard*

*was celestial music*

*Penguins have sent their*
*first representatives to the UN*

*Whale speech decoded and their*
*good counsel received*

*Firearms all over the world have*
*melted now combat is only*

*hand to hand*

*Nuclear Powers can't find their*
*warheads for their*

*warheads have vanished*

*Today no one raised their voice*
*and good words were heard by all*

A bit puerile perhaps but far
better than the usual news


6/25/2012, *Down at the Deep End*

# LITTLE SAGA OF THE MARS GARAGE

Sometimes Mars is like a large garage

The other planets come and park there for a while in order to
get out of the hurly-burly of always
careening around in orbit

They hang suspended there in the cool darkness as if to
refuel revolving more slowly surrounded by
muffling clouds

Planet Nesbeth and Ashtaroth and the original
Ygdrasil in the shape of a large mountainous comb...

Nasturtia once woke from a darkened nap to find
Scordania softly weeping over the gradual
disappearance of her inhabitants

Scordanza comforted Scordania since they were
near cousins in the galactic sphere and an
occasional star would come in for a breather and
shed bright cheerful sparkly light on the
scene of these timeless large mineral orbs as if
cooling their heels

Space in its vastness barely feels their absence
though strange puckerings take place and velvety
spatial shrinking until the planets pop back into orbit again and
all the longitudes and latitudes snap back into shape at the sound of
little whirring cogs and sweet twangings of airy
seeming nothingness

But one day Laladong the littlest planet in our system

barely a planet at all but falling into
planetary definition decided not to go back
out there in the dark and distant cold he really
wouldn't couldn't shan't and won't it's too horrible too
alien that far away from the sun no friends no
influences magnetic or otherwise

Mars was confounded with little Laladong huddled at the
back of its garage not listening to reason in its
staunch refusal to cooperate in orbital harmony

Mars trembled and shook soothingly tickled its sides together
set up a really strong vibration and even sang true
celestial music into Laladong's numerous cratered ears
but Laladong was beyond reason
something had happened out there some mysterious
trauma to cause him such fearsome grief all by
himself alone seemingly motherless and fatherless
with no mate visible or invisible to comfort and
assuage his fears until

finally Mars summoned up its ultimate in
Martian tenderness and closed in around
Laladong as if it were a warm incubating womb and

squeezed gently but firmly tighter and tighter until Laladong
experienced the height of both natal love and natal pressure and

exploded out into rebirth again as it had so many
millions of millennia earlier but now recharged with

mortality and meaning sped out into space and
clicked back into its orbit in its invincible track

whistling again its harmonious part in the
true Music of the Spheres

and Mars closed over its surface again and
turned its shy side earthwards

hiding its nurturing matronly aspect under a visage of

hard red rock and

rough inhospitable atmospheres

3/22/2004, *Mars & Beyond* (abridged)

## NOSEHAIR

Tonight, at age fifty, I cut a curling hair from my
    right nostril that bothers me, the first time in
my life a nostril hair has started to
        get out of control. What is God's
purpose in starting interior nostril hairs growing long at
half-century point? Should we have
sweeping whiskers out of our noses to look more
ferocious as we feel
    more benevolent? Do our
snout-hairs start lengthening to get us used to feeling
less handsomely heroic? As if at a
    signal, literal hair-trigger, curling
        strands out of nostrils, to show
biological surprise, to ready us for body's
inevitable toboggan ride downhill to
    hairy decrepitude? That our
eyes glitter with ignited nuggets of
    wisdom and
        compassion as old age, those bristly
wisps curling out from our
        breath-holes, overtakes us? I
can't imagine it happening to a
    teenager! This is
        old man's
business: Gaining wisdom, growing
    nose hair.


10/15/1990, *The Heart Falls in Love with Visions of Perfection*

# HOMAGE TO THE DISCOVERERS

Aroo, the short man with slight limp
who discovered the lengthening and
shortening of shadows throughout the day,

Kafnaa, woman of straight black hair and
   slim pointed breasts who saw the way to add
water to sifted flour to make sun-baked bread,
and her sister Poona who
   flattened the lumps and lay them on
      smooth hot rocks just after sunrise.
Poona also seemed to understand
      the language of cats.

Horgnath, elegantly supple and lightly
   muscled, who found a way to
sit on a horse's back and soothe it into
going where he wanted, squeezing his
   thighs and making those
      clucking and clicking noises with his
tongue you hear horse-trainers use today.

Bazna Snarr, who found that by cupping her
mouth with her hands as she stood on a
   rocky outcrop, her voice carried
      a little farther to Shnoog waiting on
the opposite cliff, cupping his ear the same way,
   nearly out of sight behind a
      stand of tall pines,

Tash, who made the discovery that a
   crushed bug never walks,

Tos, that water poured onto an incline will
  roll down it rather than
    stay in a puddle on its angle
(certainly the spiritual and probable
  genetic ancestor to Newton millenniums later),

Oolash, who found that by putting berries
  between two rocks and squeezing, he'd
    get juice, of course, he
had to lick the rocks, receptacles discovered not
    until some time later, by

Shla, by making a depression in soft clay
with an egg, preferably a petrified egg,
then letting the clay sit in the sun until hard,
then catching the juice as
  discovered by Oolash that runs down an
incline as discovered by Tos, and
raising the clay cup of juice to
Chief Katoosh, a form of celebration

discovered by Yoloff one twilight
  evening under an
    aurora borealis sky

*ah*, all these are our ancestors in discovery
the way babies discover staircases and
  hot pans, sunlight on their
    faces and
      mosquito bites,

and their active shadows still fall this far
along in time –

Jaja who discovered that by
sitting on a flat piece of bark he could
    toboggan down a hill,

Smoonash who discovered that by putting
a small block of ice (even better splattered with
fresh berry juice) on a stick,
  he had the first popsicle,

or Laniah who saw the figures and objects
  in dreams and knew they had
    sinister or positive import,

firstness and freshness being the
key to our own lightheartedness

while a mushroom cloud rises behind us
and technological doom gently
    tugs at our clothes

to sit down among its discoveries

like looming
shadows on a wall.


12/19/1997, *You Open a Door and It's a Starry Night*

## THE MAN WITH TWO HEADS

Once there was a man with two heads
they worked independently of each other and
everything went smoothly for the most part

one was named Robert and the other was named
Robert and though they resembled each other to the
swan-like eyebrows and cheekbones like
Mt. Rushmore and blue eyes that were
turquoise-brown in every light but green
there were significant differences

Moonlight falls on Robert's face while sleeping
he wakes behind a waterfall of blue moonlight

Sunlight discharges its golden rays on Robert's face
like bronze medallions tossed in the air and coming down
rain he is always in the picture
he is always in sharp focus while

Robert on the other hand is damp and wobbly
as if cut from felt and
pressed against a low window

The rose tree survived his meek inheritance
sudden accelerations propelled the interior
Roberts ahead of their exteriors

They would discuss matters in matter-of-fact tones
under bridges on rooftops in high wind
the two of them

Robert had a moustache and Robert had a moustache that
neither of them liked
*"Why don't you shave that dead
caterpillar off your lip?"*
The other snickered *"I'll be around
long before you're gone"*

The three of them two heads one body circumlocuted
every circumstance the world flashed by and
they saw no reason to come to even a
gentlemen's disagreement to disagree
or make any adjustment to co-exist in imperfect
harmony or come to simple terms with
things-as-they-are which is the
usual situation as we walk superstitiously under
ladders expecting the sky to fall on us Praise the
Lord Knock on wood
*"Come in!"* So

Robert and his namesake ceased speaking to each
other altogether and one would just let the
other order over-rich food or pay
too much at the department store or
say everything wrong with ecstatic self-
confidence thinking to himself *"It'll show him!"*
forgetting his own intimate connection for a
moment to the outcome

Robert's inner vision of himself was a
giraffe's head placidly picking fresh top leaves and
contentedly chewing green leaves in late
bronze African sunlight

Robert's other inner vision of himself or
other Robert's version of self (his) was
flagellant and flatter earth-flat elevator
up elevator down but never getting
definitively off at any floor for sure

It was a tertial complexity
complexification never-ending
this two-headed man who looked for all
intents and purposes as normal as a flea
yet two heads jutted from a polished collar
two hands gestured from two polished cuffs

He moved among us smiling-frowning happy-sad
sexy-sexless both in the identical instant

He sits in a hole and covers his head in the
dream this morning with monster cobwebs

He rapidly glides along tracks of slick iridescence in those
elusive thoughts you thought you'd never
think

Robert Robert
O Robert with two heads both named
Robert


2/23/2000, *Shaking the Quicksilver Pool*

# POEM IN THE FIRST PERSON

*Wait!* Before you begin a new poem
do you really want to add yet one

more to the planet's population of unread poems?
Are you so sure what emerges will be

among the read ones the ones in their
own daylight aboveground leading

happy lives as part of the melodious family of
read or at least skimmed over or even

half-heartedly glanced at poems?

Those of us who are among the unread
have to hang out in neon-lit 24 hour diners or

hospital emergency rooms in case someone
somewhere might turn to us or happen upon us

and begin reading silently to themselves or
on a good night or day

even read us out loud
*(I'm thrilled at the prospect!)*

We all have to be on call and all our
ducks in a row so to speak in

readiness but you should know
we're the Silent Majority we poems

gorgeously written but
never read

I don't want to discourage you and
getting read may not be

uppermost in your mind as you set out yet again
through the beast-ridden savage forest of a

new poem

Maybe for you a poem being
alive anywhere under

moonlit clouds in a haunted purple
landscape with wide-eyed creatures is

enough and if someone should actually
turn on a light and read it and it flowers into full

Technicolor and sense-surround sound well
*bravo!*

And if it stays in a
dark drawer as so many of us did for so

long with Emily's tidy
ribboned bundles that's

Okay too –
Go ahead!

Write on!

God speed

*and good luck!*


10/17/2001, *The Match That Becomes a Conflagration*

On Writing Poetry

## WHY DOES THE SOUL LOVE POETRY?

1

Out of all possibility,
    why does the soul love
        poetry? Why does a jet of black
            spout up from
        depths usually ignored?

At the sound of words precisely placed, at the
rub of sonorous edges, reverberations that
dislodge something usually asleep?

Rubies glimmer in drab cinderblock walls,
dragonfly wings scintillate their
        oil and water shimmer. Dusk has
fallen and people have become more serious,
the night is coming on and laughter has become more
thoughtful with the coming dark.

Birds are still. Eyes are closed. Shutters also.
Hearts are opening.

2

A lone singer on a stone
    leaves his throat open to
        deepest breezes.
In his eyes hurt catches fire, longings
    conflagrate. Voices from distant horizons
gather and become visible. Dark-maned

horses are churning in white-flecked sea-surf.
No silence for miles around. All the elements

pour through the singer's song.
Even the stone he sits on
    begins to long for its
        geological home.

3

Element of the elements, the soul
    has ears for what
our usual flat daily cycles
        cannot satisfy. Where eyes see

straight boulevards, high-rise buildings,
plate-glass consistencies, the soul in its
    glowing grotto moves toward the
        magnet of earth's deepest groans,

flying fireflies of the divine lightness of being, of

stars drunk in their starry deeps, and the soul

shakes off its millennial sleep and
rises perceptibly to greet them. Above the
human clearing – mortal bodies moving around in the
half-light down below – the song-drenched

soul begins to flow upward.

4/26/1990, *A Maddening Disregard for the Passage of Time*

# CLOUD SERIES

I hate flying in airplanes, but I love writing poems in the air.
A head start, inspiration above clouds, you feel
light blue angels' lips just at your ear, mouthing
    incredible mysteries about
        angles of light, slants of beams, textures of
            glare, and
outside the floating window above Colorado you get an
idea of their meaning, blinding silver flashes in a
steady state throughout the
    upper atmosphere. Angels'
faces blend with a similar complexion into such
holy brightness. We

are heading through mountains of clouds with the
best intentions for safe arrival, but at
any moment our course might be
    abruptly interrupted to travel one of their
smoother flights, bodiless,
immortally jet-propelled, no

scrubbed bright faces of distant singing crowded at
porthole windows, no
air-pocket bumps and grinds 3,500 feet up, but

way beyond human altitudes,
The Angel of Right Now taken flight into Forever's air.


6/22/1990, *The Heart Falls in Love with Visions of Perfection* (extract)

## TO WRITE A POEM

To write a poem is to cast a net into a
    sea of ink,
the wind is howling and you can
    barely be heard
        rehearsing the lines.

Or you're in a coffin, a plain wooden affair,
people sit around you, and you've written something on the
back of a 3x5 card and are
trying to get someone to read it, sitting up,
    handing it out, an attendant
laying you back down again, sliding the card,
unread, back into your stiff and colorless
    hand, well, obviously unread!
You're supposed to be dead!

Writing a poem is getting on the back of a
giant beast of night, huffing and
        shaggy, it
    bellows off into the dark, you
        clutching its muscle, holding on for
dear life to its hide.

Hide and seek with an astronomer, an
    obstetrician, an archaeologist and a
lounge singer, in a room full of
        different sized chairs, at the
end of an abandoned pier, and you're
it, and the others have gone!

Writing a poem is a love letter to the world, to
people you've known and people you've

never known, waving out the
car window as you pass them.

I don't even know if I should have begun this
self-conscious list, feeling
   trapped by it, enclosed in my
own form and trying to
bang my way out, or
seduce the guard somehow into
      opening the cell door to
let me out. Yet, once out, I
just know I'll commit the crime and
get myself locked in again, as

fast as I can!

Writing a poem is
licking the jam off the pastry as
nonchalantly as possible. It's a High

Society Party, after all, and you never know

who'll be watching!


5/23/1999, *I Imagine a Lion*

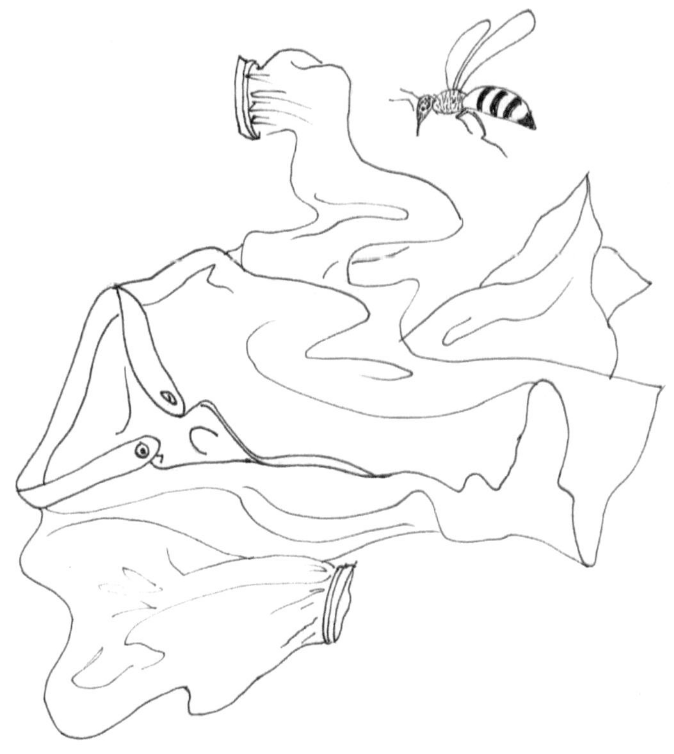

Narrative Poems

# THE CLOTH THAT REFUSED TO BE WASHED

Once upon a time someone wove a piece of cloth
but when they had it made into a shirt and
wore it then wanted to wash it
it refused to be washed
it struggled and curled and flapped and finally
flew away like newspaper in the wind
and came down on a rock resolutely refusing to let
water touch it

The man who had made the shirt didn't
know what to do
he looked with confusion at the cloth then tried
various methods to get it washed
even sneaking up on it from behind with a
bucket of hot sudsy water
splashing it on the cloth as it lay on the rock
but before the water could hit it that
stubborn sly and canny cloth curled away and the
water washed the rock instead the cloth
crumpled in more dirt at its base

In fact it got dirtier and dirtier and absolutely
no amount of stealth could overtake its
refusal to get washed
the man was shirtless
he had to wear the shirt dirty or not
he shook it brushed it snapped it in the air to
shake off the dirt but naturally the
cloth which was white to begin with began to
lose its whiteness to a whole rainbow history of
spills and mishaps and the natural
rubbing against the soiled walls of life

until the shirt really was a flag of
the past almost like a map of its owner's
actions and reactions foibles weaknesses and darkness
cat-hair a grease spot a coffee stain one little
patch of the original whiteness but no longer a
brilliant white which it could get if it only would
submit to some hot water and soap
that pristine original state of the present
which would redeem it from its past and give it a
future perhaps I'm getting a little too
theological here but at any rate

One day the shirt was hanging on a hook and getting
progressively left behind by the man who made another
shirt out of an old sheet which allowed the weekly
washing without protest

and a rosy shirt went by in the dark corner where the old shirt
hung a bright flowered red and green and purple
splashy print affair that excited the cloth of the
once-white shirt until it wriggled and wrenched and finally
flipped off of its hook and with a kind of
textile longing in its warp and woof
dragged itself across the
dirt floor of the poor man's hut...

and managed to knock down a glass of water that had been
left on the floor by one of the man's
children and lay there as the water
splashed on an edge enough to
wet it completely and even wash away at least a
tiny fraction of its dirt
for love of the flowery shirt
for love of its roses red and green and purple

It never saw that shirt again but it
waited for it every time the man wore it
gleaming white again at the market or in the
village square the white shirt keeping its
eye out for the other one to pass by
the eye of its buttonhole perhaps
I don't know
the eye of its simple consciousness of itself as a
shirt and not a
sewing machine

the shirt that refused to get washed until its
reason for refusal evaporated
for a greater love than itself

until it grew old and threadbare and got
patched and re-sewn and new
buttons put on and then made into
patches itself on a full ruffly skirt for his wife and found itself
next to a patch that had
red and green and purple roses on it

*It was finally united with its beloved!*

and the wind blew through them and

rippled and rustled them both as his
wife worked or danced or walked to the marketplace

or threw it in a heap for washing
as she appeared to her husband naked as light

as clean as the day she was born

as clean as a cloth that's submitted to washing

in the darkened room.

1/24/2000, *Millennial Prognostications* (abridged)

# THE BLIND BEEKEEPER

*for Musa Muhaiyaddeen*

1

I'd like to make a movie entitled
  *"The Blind Beekeeper."* Alphonse,
or it could be Henry, blinded by sparks from a
forge when a teenager on his family farm
circa 1943, walks like a man on the moon
(funny how the phrase "man in the moon"
   predated the historical event probably by
      centuries) toward his white
wooden bee sanctuaries,

he's wearing no protective suit or headdress,
knows the mental workings of bees,
   can call them individually by
      name, they swarm onto him, if
         that's the right term, they
cover his torso, stripped as he is to the waist,
his face wreathed in smiles,

and he does the dance of the bee with
bees all over him, like a bee pin cushion,
this man against a green field on a
      sunny Kansas afternoon, the
         camera rises in a
spectacular crane shot of Henry
      shrinking smaller and
         smaller, black with
bees, calling each one by name, his

voice on the sound track, each time he
repeats a new name, there's an increased
   buzz response, the music of the
soundtrack is a single violin note,

the sun's beating down, suddenly there's a
flash of light

and in the place of Henry and his bees
there's a large jar of honey, almost white,
as if from Paradise, glowing like a
   pot of gold.

All of this could take place before the
   credits.

Now the story begins.

2

We are taken into the bee's world.
Zarzz (all the bees have names starting with
   "Z") has progressive ideas,
he's been to France, feels independent,
   wants to revolutionize the bees'
      lives, thinks about
breaking out of the routine and
   starting his own hive, saves up
pollen secretly in some abandoned
   hexagons in a nearby field,
is in love with Zuzz, wants to
make her his queen.

Zarzz, although commendable on

one level for being a
   bee who wants to make a difference,
doesn't appreciate the divine pattern involved
in being a bee. That there's only
   so far you can go before you
betray beedom, or, potentially tragic in this case,
build, not so much castles in the air, as
hives in hell. But his
   intentions start out as good.

He's in love, he has some thoughts on
improving the lot of bees, but his
   radical ideas might ruin this
hive forever!

Enter the blind beekeeper. He wants to
   learn the higher metaphysics of
bees, to touch with the
   knowledge of his heart the
geometric perfection of the bee, its
almost symbolically ritualistic sets of
   patterns, building patterns, dance
patterns, whose results are
deep medicine for man, prophetically
   ordained, and
the continuation of the species. The

flash he experienced that
   blinded him he wants to
reproduce in the realm of spiritual
   illumination.

Meanwhile Zarzz and Zuzz leave the
   hive in search of

greener pastures. They pack up their
legs with pollen, and head out after
sunset. But bees don't
  fly after dark. They get lost.
They fly into foreign fields. They get
  cold, which is
    fatal for the
      flying mechanism of bees, who
have to keep themselves warm by whirring their
wings. Their story gets quite sad, actually,
and Zarzz suddenly realizes he may have
  doomed both their lives to
    extinction. Being a
thoughtful bee, he is wracked with
guilt and worry, and
starts to pray, for bees are believers,
  as attested to by the beginning of that
word, and have a

beeline to the Divine Reality Who
gave them their wisdom.

3

Zarzz: Zee zuzz za za-za-za
  zarzi zuzzo zab zuzzo
    zizz za za-za zarzo zoo.

Zuzz: Zarzi zaz zaz zo-zo-zo-zo-zo
  ziz zar zuzzo zizz zo zo za-za
    zazizzo zazizzo.

Zarzz: Zazo zizo zizz?

Zuzz: Zazo zinzinzup zardo-do zinzanzo
   zar zar.

Zarzz: Zee Zuzz, za zwa zi za zo.

4

But the beekeeper is also in love, and he
   also wants to build hexagons of
      perfection and a palace of
         pure sweetness.
Her name is Rosa, a poor girl from a
   foreign country, and Henry is
her strength and she is his eyes.

But here is the strange part: as Henry
works with the bees, and talks to
   them in their language,
he starts seeing them, visually
seeing each one of them. When he's away from their
hive he's blind, but when he faces the
hive he's an alchemist achieving pure gold.

He comes to the hive in the morning.
The hive is in an uproar. He sees them in
clusters talking about Zarzz and Zuzz.
The queen is laying her eggs. The
nurses are taking them to the nursery.
At the center of the hive everything is

going on as normal. But out in the
streets the bees are literally abuzz.
*"What will we do? What have they
   gone and done? Where could they*

*have gone? How can we get them back?"*

The blind beekeeper looks into the hive
and sees all this. But suddenly he has
double sight. He sees Zarzz and Zuzz
nearly frozen to death, trying to
sun themselves enough to fly. They are
in a field a few miles away
   bounded by meadow flowers.

There's no time to lose! The beekeeper
calls to the bees. Their round shiny
   multiple eyes all turn to him.
He dances. He dances the dance of
   the map to the field they're in.
He turns in circles to indicate miles. He faces
   in their direction. He tilts
   his arms to show the longitude and
      latitude of their
         position.

Now he calls each one by name to
   go to them, to bring them back: *"Go
Zuza, Zee, Zan, Zy,
   Zarzo, Zeeza, Zanzan, Zink,
go Zeno, Zardoz, Zo, Zooey,
   Zap, Zeeper, Zazoo, Zip,
go Zeezee, Zantham, Zoetrope, Zany,
   Zeke, Zap, Zazz, Zoe,
Zanzinzo, Zoonzinzan, Zeezay, Zope,
go Zaza, Zipe!* They buzz their response!
*Go Zak, z-z-z-z, Zook, z-z-z-z,
   Zipper, z-z-z-z, Zay!*

They lift from the hive like an ecstatic
        cloud, they buzz like chainsaws
and off they zoom. The blind
    beekeeper smiles and waves them
        on. Does the story end happily?

They all burst into song!

5

Zarzz and Zuzz come back to the hive.
Everyone's glad they're still alive.

The queen makes Zarzz her intimate vizier.
Zuzz marries Zarzz and gets busier and busier.

The blind beekeeper makes lots of money
selling their extraordinary honey

and marries Rosa in a flash of light
so utterly intense he regains his sight.


2/2/1996, *The Blind Beekeeper*

On Death & Dying

# FANCY DANCER

This cancer I've been dancing with
(and cancer's a fancy dancer)
has overcome its scruples
and wants to marry me

I've rebuffed it once or twice now
but its piteous face puckers
and tears fill its eyes
with the thought of losing me

I'm almost past objecting
so I must take some time
(not to think it over
no time for that)

but to prepare for our love bed
in the depths of our deepest love nest
in as great a comfort as possible
for the long duration


2/21/2016, *Holy Door in the Ground*

# WHEN A PERSON DIES

*In Memoriam Joe Rudolph*

1

When a person dies he leaves the
    domain of the air
        for the domain of the heart, our
heart, the heart of his closest ones, his
own heart. Disappears in it. Sinking

upward. Diving gear the
    void, open space, the majestic
        silence between stars. The single

silence that outspreads
    all. Just

slips away. And into our
own hearts goes, tipping his

hat even more
    nonchalantly than before, making those
fleeting facial expressions to himself and to
    us all the more
        easily, the radiant
spectrum from the face of being
alone to the face put on for anyone,
    single or multiple, other than
himself and God. The face put on for
God the same as a
    lake wears early

mornings. Catching
    earliest
        rays.

2

Goes into the heart with its ventricles of white mist
from the domain of the air where
gulping sunflowers turn their heads, the fishbowl in which
every living thing breathes, suspended on
air as on spatial hooks, oxygen tree that hangs
downward into our physical beings with its
nourishing branches breathing our bodies,
structure of matter held in
living nets of air. We swim out of our
mother's wombs into its ocean,
we move like aerialists across its
high expanse, spotlit against night's
    tent-roof.
On high peaks and low desert we
    gasp for air like little
        flesh automobiles running out of gas,
we wear air on the inside like the
    name of our true love,
we extend ourselves across it by means of
    secret signals agreed upon beforehand
whose cipher is the pure light we
    breathe in concert with every
        breathing being,
inside out – Klein-Bottle reality! In air we
move, with air inside
    us, it being our

real flesh. Our own flesh the
white flag of total surrender we pin on our
    sinking bones.


3


When we die we go from fishbowl to auricle,
no longer air-creature we become heart-creature
   entire, moving in its haunted landscapes of
     antiquity and futurity, seeing all the
prophetic faces pass us in corridors of sorrow,
palisades of joy. It's all here. Rushing
   flood of grief in the survivors
     become dripping faucet in the heart from which
drops appear with a photographic image of the dead one's face
perfectly centered in each one,
lighting up in the air now of the heart like a
spark that flies from Void to
   Emptiness by way of an


arc'd moment of living incandescence.
Going quickly into the heart again, taking on


majestic form, the orchestra of passing states
responding to the baton of a fly


arched in the air like an eyebrow.


Gone from the air into a
   shimmering cry in moonlight by
     train tracks extending past physical matter,
gone from the air into a spinning sphere atop a
    silver pole of pure sound,

gone into the heart of two caves opening out on
        double infinities,
gone into the heart of distinct planetary motions, as
     definite as speech, dialog of
ecstatic molecules,

inside out to this world on a horse of fiery thought
    that leaps from
burning roof to roof with the greatest of
         ease,

gone into the heart bigger than the universe,
elegant breeze scented with deep garden spices,
evening light stained by a sunset's glow,
arctic dawn, like a single shattering crystal.

They go from us, the dead,
   and the heart
      encloses them.
They go from us, and the
   light

stands where they stood.


2/20/1992, *Orpheus Meets Morpheus*[6]

---

6    Dedicated to Tasneem Vandenberg 2001 – 2022.

## HORSE

*for Sahar von Schlegell, in memory of her father*

"*Bring me my horse!*"
"Father, you have no horse.
We sold it to pay for your funeral.
Besides, we couldn't get it up the
    stairs five flights."

"*Then bring me my transistor radio.*"
"Father, that too is gone. We
    had to buy food for your
last days on earth. We had to buy
medicines."

"*The days are long, the winds are
    strong. My own father's
extending his hand. Through
traffic noise and rock'n'roll
my ancestors are extending
    their hands.*"
"Father, the room is dark
and the gypsies have died.
Here's garlic and bright cloth,
here's a clock with its
hands torn off, and the
plastic melted."

"*Bring me the carton of snapshots.
I want to gaze at them
    one last time, and
        say goodbye.*"
"They too are gone, when the

house burned down."

*"Then bring me my wife. I'll
look on her sweet face again."*
"Ah, dear father, she left us last year,
and waits on the other side of the
river for you, all dressed in
white, standing above black water."

*"Is there nothing at all to bring your father,
is the world so poor and I so poor
there's nothing at all to bring?"*
"We brought it all, and it was
nothing. All webs, and cobwebs,
entangled in webs. What you want now,
    father, is unentangled
and free."

*"Then bring me your faces, one by one, to
    kiss goodbye."*
"Here, dear father, is a forehead,
here a warm cheek. Your lips are
    cold, father, the room is dark."

*"Bring me my horse. With the golden
    saddle. I will
ride it now."*

"Here's your horse, dear father.
Here's your horse."

1/20/1999, *You Open a Door and It's a Starry Night*

## DEATH IS COMING

Death is coming
and we're going to have a

lawn party
though it be winter

I'm going to wear my hat

The wheels of earth are
revolving with a grinding sound

I can make out death's face
in the mist

How can I believe it
with light all around?

Not even a little door
is needed that's how fully

dimensional I feel and
green shoots growing in space

everywhere at once
in the winter chill


1/4/2008, *The Fire Eater's Lunchbreak*

# I'M GOING TO THE HOLY DOORWAY

I'm going to the
holy doorway in the

ground

It opens up before you know
you've gone

windows here are
blackened over

each one with its
moon

there no windows separate you
from His

Throne

conversation dazzles like a
flock of birds

and every word is God's
reverberation

and every word hits
heart-chords in the

clouds of our being

Everything here says "goodbye"
in the midst of

seeing it

There enlightenment is reached by
simply being it

I've sat among the saints and
heard their

silence rise

Lord may my silence

join theirs in Your

Eyes


2/17/2016, #59, *Transitioning to Zero*

## ONLY ALLAH

I was born in a hospital in
Alameda California

*Only Allah*

I had this face I
have even now

*Only Allah*

The lights crisscrossed
this way and that

*Only Allah*

My parents loved each other
and showed affection

*Only Allah*

I drew pictures on
construction paper

*Only Allah*

The door swung open and
I went through it

*Only Allah*

Sat as a Buddhist
facing a wall

*Only Allah*

Wrote *Dawn Visions* on a
trip to Mexico

*Only Allah*

San Francisco
1964

*Only Allah*

Angel Gabriel
stood up in a tree

*Only Allah*

The Floating Lotus
Magic Opera Company

*Only Allah*

A Sufi shaykh's
deputy in an

attic room in Berkeley

*Only Allah*

Shaykh ibn al-Habib
in Meknes Morocco

*Only Allah*

Clouds rolled away
and keep rolling away

*Only Allah*

Drove with five others
in a Peugeot in Algeria

*Only Allah*

Met saints of Allah there
Hajj Isa ben Hajj Isa and Hajj Isa

*Only Allah*

Married Malika in a
burst of light

*Only Allah*

Came to Philadelphia
where Bawa's gaze covers us

*Only Allah*

The *Deen* of Islam a garden
with living vegetation

*Only Allah*

Shaping us into
alchemical human beings

*Only Allah*

Cancer *zamzam* hemp oil
wheat grass

*Only Allah*

The Door of Light
with a Dark Door inside it

*Only Allah*

The Door of Dark
with a Light Door inside it

*Only Allah*

Being here for a moment
going on forever

*Only Allah*

*La ilaha illa Allah
Muhammad Rasulullah*


7/17/2015, *White Noise in This World Silver in the Next*

# STARBATTLE BRILLIANT[7]

A pearlescent papyrus appeared out of

sheer nothingness

held over an abyss of brilliance

and whose speech was an ocean of

silence articulate to the last

wave dissolved against a sizzling

night of deepest blackness

innermostly and outermostly

manifest as light in our

eyes and hearts in Allah's

Perfect Sight forever


3/13/2016, *Holy Door in the Ground*

---

7    This was Abdal-Hayy's last poem.

## COMPLETE WORKS

### POETRY

- *Dawn Visions* (City Lights Books, San Francisco, 1964)

- *This Body of Black Light Gone Through the Diamond* (Fred Stone, Cambridge, Mass., 1965)

- *On the Streets at Night Alone* (1965?)

- *All Hail the Surgical Lamp* (1967)

- *States of Amazement* (1970)

- *Burnt Heart /Ode to the War Dead* (City Lights Books, San Francisco, 1972)

- *The Chronicles of Akhira* (1981) (Zilzal Press, Philadelphia, with typoglyphs by Karl Kempton, 1986)

- *Mouloud* (1984) (Zilzal Press chapbook, Philadelphia, 1995)

- *Man Is the Crown of Creation* (1984) (The Ecstatic Exchange, 2012, published as *The Crown of Creation*, with illustrations by the author)

- *The Look of the Lion* (The Parabolas of Sight) (1984)

- *The Desert Is the Only Way Out* (completed 4/21/1984) (Zilzal Press chapbook, Philadelphia, 1985)

- *Atomic Dance* (1984) (am here books, Santa Barbara, 1988)

- *Outlandish Tales* (1984)

- *Awake as Never Before* (12/26/1984) (Zilzal Press chapbook, Philadelphia, 1993)

- *Glorious Intervals* (1/1/1985) (Zilzal Press chapbook, Philadelphia, date unknown)

- *Long Days on Earth/Book I* (1985)

- *Long Days on Earth/Book II (Hayy Ibn Yaqzan)* (1985)

- *Long Days on Earth/Book III* (1986)

- *Long Days on Earth/Book IV* (1986)

- *The Ramadan Sonnets (Long Days on Earth/Book V)* (1986) (published by Jusoor-Kitab/City Lights Books, West Bethesda/San Francisco, 1996; republished as *Ramadan Sonnets* by The Ecstatic Exchange, 2005)

- *Long Days on Earth/Book VI* (1986)

- *Halley's Comet* (Zilzal Press, Philadelphia, 1986)

- *Holograms* (9/4/1986 – 3/26/1987)

- *History of the World (The Epic of Man's Survival)* (4/7 – 6/18/1987)

- *Exploratory Odes* (6/25 – 10/18/1987)

- *The Man at the End of the World* (11/11 – 12/10/1987)

- *Fed From Underground Springs* (7/30 – 11/23/1988)

- *Atomic Dance* (1984) (am here books, Santa Barbara, 1988)

- *Ideas of the Heart* (11/27/1988 – 5/5/1989)

- *New Poems* (scattered poems out of series, from 3/24 – 8/9/1989)

- *The Heart Falls In Love With Visions of Perfection* (6/15/1990 – 6/2/1991)

- *Orpheus Meets Morpheus* (8/1/1991 – 3/14/1992)

- *The Greater Vehicle* (10/17/1993 – 4/30/1994)

- *The Quest for Beauty* – illustrated by Sara Steele (Zilzal Press, Philadelphia, 1994)

- *Roses, A Selection of Poems* (Zilzal Press, Philadelphia, 1994)

- *The Angel Broadcast* (9/29 – 12/17/1995)

- *Mecca/Medina Time-Warp* (Zilzal Press, Philadelphia, 1996)

- *Flight to Egypt* (5/1 – 5/16/1999)

- *The Blind Beekeeper* (Zilzal Press chapbook, Philadelphia, 1999; republished by Jusoor/Syracuse University Press, Syracuse, 2001)

- *Mars & Beyond* (poems written 1/2 – 4/29/2004) (The Ecstatic Exchange, 2005)

- *Ramadan Sonnets* (The Ecstatic Exchange, 2005)

- *Salt Prayers* (poems written 5/29 – 10/24/1998) (The Ecstatic Exchange, 2005)

- *Laughing Buddha Weeping Sufi* (11/7/2003 – 1/10/2004) (The Ecstatic Exchange, 2005)

- *Psalms for the Brokenhearted* (1/22 – 5/25/2003) (The Ecstatic Exchange, 2006)

- *I Imagine a Lion* (5/21 – 11/15/1999) (The Ecstatic Exchange, 2006)

- *Coattails of the Saint* (The Ecstatic Exchange, 2006)

- *Love is a Letter Burning in a High Wind* (9/21 – 11/6/2003) (The Ecstatic Exchange, 2006)

- *Abdallah Jones and the Disappearing-Dust Caper* (The Ecstatic Exchange, 2006)

- *The Flame of Transformation Turns to Light/Ninety-Nine Ghazals Written in English* (5/14 – 8/21/2002) (The Ecstatic Exchange, 2007)

- *Underwater Galaxies* (The Ecstatic Exchange, 2007)

- *The Music Space* (2001) (The Ecstatic Exchange, 2007)

- *Cooked Oranges* (7/23/2004 – 1/24/2005) (The Ecstatic Exchange, 2007)

- *Through Rose Colored Glasses* (The Ecstatic Exchange, 2008)

- *Like When You Wave at a Train and the Train Hoots Back at You/Farid's Book* (11/6 – 26/7 and 6-9/11/1991) (The Ecstatic Exchange, 2008)

- *In the Realm of Neither* (2006) (The Ecstatic Exchange, 2008)

- *The Fire Eater's Lunchbreak* (11/11/2007 – 5/19/2008) (The Ecstatic Exchange, 2008)

- *Millennial Prognostications* (11/25/1999 – 2/2/2000) (The Ecstatic Exchange, 2008)

- *Hoopoe's Argument* (5/27 – 9/18/2003)

- *You Open a Door and It's a Starry Night* (10/29/1997 – 5/23/1998) (The Ecstatic Exchange, 2009)

- *Where Death Goes* (The Ecstatic Exchange, 2009)

- *Shaking the Quicksilver Pool* (The Ecstatic Exchange, 2009)

- *The Perfect Orchestra* (3/30 – 7/25/1988) (The Ecstatic Exchange, 2009)

- *Sparrow on the Prophet's Tomb* (The Ecstatic Exchange, 2009)

- *A Maddening Disregard for the Passage of Time* (11/17/1989 – 5/20/1990) (The Ecstatic Exchange, 2009)

- *Stretched Out on Amethysts* (The Ecstatic Exchange, 2010)

- *Invention of the Wheel* (11/13/2006 – 6/10/2007) (The Ecstatic Exchange, 2010)

- *Sparks off the Main Strike* (5/24/2008 – 1/10/2009) (The Ecstatic Exchange, 2010)

- *Chants for the Beauty Feast* (The Ecstatic Exchange, 2011)

- *In Constant Incandescence* (2/10 – 8/13/2010) (The Ecstatic Exchange, 2011)

- *Holiday from the Perfect Crime* (1/25 – 6/11/2005) (The Ecstatic Exchange, 2011)

- *The Caged Bear Spies the Angel* (The Ecstatic Exchange, 2011)

- *The Puzzle* (3/21/1992 – 8/17/1993) (The Ecstatic Exchange, 2011)

- *This Light Slants Upward* (3/7 – 10/13/2011)

- *Ramadan Is Burnished Sunlight* (part of *This Light Slants Upward*, published separately, The Ecstatic Exchange, 2011)

- *Ala-udeen & The Magic Lamp* (with illustrations by the author) (The Ecstatic Exchange, 2011)

- *Blood Songs* (The Ecstatic Exchange, 2012), winner of a 2013 American Book Award

- *Down at the Deep End* (The Ecstatic Exchange, 2012)

- *Next Life* (8/9/2012 – 2/12/2013) (The Ecstatic Exchange, 2013)

- *A Hundred Little 3D Pictures* (5/14/1994 – 9/11/1995) (The Ecstatic Exchange, 2013)

- *Miracle Songs for the Millennium* (1/23 – 10/16/1996) (The Ecstatic Exchange, 2014)

- *Some* (10/25/1998 – 4/25/1999) (The Ecstatic Exchange, 2014)

- *The Throne Perpendicular to All That is Horizontal* (9/18/2009 – 1/25/2010) (The Ecstatic Exchange, May 2014)

- *He Comes Running: A Turkish Sojourn, and Myths We Never Knew* (November 2013) (The Ecstatic Exchange, September 2014)

- *The Soul's Home* (2/13 – 10/8/2013) (The Ecstatic Exchange, December 2014)

- *Stories Too Fiery to Sing Too Watery to Whisper* (6/13 – 10/24/2005) (The Ecstatic Exchange, December 2014)

- *The Sweet Enigma of It All* (The Ecstatic Exchange, 2014)

- *The Sound of Geese over the House* (6/15 – 11/4/2007) (The Ecstatic Exchange, 2015)

- *Let Me See Diamonds Everywhere I Look* (6/18/2014 – 1/15/2015)

- *With Every Breath* (1/18/2015 – unfinished)

- *White Noise in This World Silver in the Next* (The Ecstatic Exchange, 2015)
- *The Match That Becomes a Conflagration* (10/14/2011 – 4/9/2012) (The Ecstatic Exchange, 2016)
- *Transitioning to Zero* (2016) (The Ecstatic Exchange, 2018)
- *Holy Door in the Ground* (2016) (The Ecstatic Exchange, 2018)

## THEATER / THE FLOATING LOTUS MAGIC OPERA COMPANY

- *The Walls are Running Blood* (1968)
- *Bliss Apocalypse* (1970)
- *The New York Ramayana* (commissioned by Lotus Music & Dance), 2000
- *Rainforest* (date unknown)

## PUPPET THEATER

- *The Mystical Romance of Layla & Majnun* (2000)
- *Ameen's Journey to Qalbiyya* (2004)

## COMPILATION OF QUOTES

- *Warrior Wisdom* (Running Press, 1993)

## PROSE

- *Zen Rock Gardening* (as Abd al-Hayy Moore, Running Press, 1992)
- *The Little Book of Zen* (as Daniel Moore, illustrated by Michael Green), (Lawrence Teacher Publishing Group, 2001)
- *Zen Wisdom: Magnetic Quotes and Proverbs* (as Daniel Moore, Cider Mill Press, 2006)

# ACKNOWLEDGMENTS

So many people have contributed in some way to helping with the manifestation of this manuscript, and I wish to thank each one!

I must start with my children, Mukhtar Sanders, Farid Sanders, and Salihah Moore, each of whom have unique and special talents and abilities that proved to be very useful.

Mukhtar, for his skills and experience in book production (one of the mainstays of his work at his graphic design company in London, Inspiral Design.) Many thanks to Mukhtar for his advice, and especially for formatting the manuscript!

Farid, many thanks for your business acumen and wisdom, particularly in suggesting that we go with Launchgood to raise money for the production costs. He was our practical voice for the business side of our project.

To Salihah, I am so thankful for her artistic vision for the project, as well as for her clear-minded and heartfelt support in helping with making decisions. We formed a great group of co-workers!

We thank Chris Blauvelt of Launchgood for seeing us through our campaign to raise the necessary funds for the production. And of course, many thanks to the folks from all over the world who contributed to the Launchgood Campaign, especially our executive producer and "Angel in a Starry Overcoat," Ibrahim Tahir of Wardah Books, Singapore!

To our dear friend, brother, uncle, and mentor Haroon Sugich, many, many thanks for his wise counsel, advice, guidance, and help!

And to Zak Whiteman for the beautiful video he produced for the fundraising effort. Blessings and thanks also to Abdal-Latif Whiteman for the cool music composition that accompanied the video!

We are grateful, too, to Myra Diaz for helping to proofread this manuscript, for her abiding friendship and support, and for her suggestions for the Category illustrations. Also many thanks to Sarah Aschenbach for doing the final proofreading.

Thanks also to Lateefa Spiker for her beautiful contributions to the artwork! And Larry Didona for his help with the scans of the artwork for the category pages.

But far and away, the biggest thanks must go to our amazing publicist and editor, Medina Tenour Whiteman! My children and I consider it to be a kind of miracle that we got her on board to foster and promote the works of my husband, which she does by posting them on social media, as well as hosting podcasts and online poetry parties on his behalf! Medina is very much a brilliant poet in her own right and has long been a fan of Abdal-Hayy's work. In fact, he was her mentor, and published her first book of poems, Love is a Traveller and We are Its Path.

Suffice it to say that Medina certainly did most of the work in bringing this manuscript together, although we had many long, but joyful, hours of working together as well, in London, Paris, and on international Zoom fests, poring over Abdal-Hayy's poems and making the selections.

It truly has been a labor of Love!

MALIKA MOORE
*August 18, 2021*

# CATEGORY ARTWORK CREDITS

**DANIEL ABDAL-HAYY MOORE**

Heart Wisdom (from *Burnt Heart*, City Lights Book, 1971)
The Imaginal World
Ecstatic Love (held in his Archive at Bancroft Library, UC Berkeley)
Funny Poems

**MALIKA MOORE**

Animals & Nature (inspired by classical Islamic drawings of animals)
Ramadan
Mawlid Poems (inspired by classical Islamic devotional art)
Family
On Writing Poetry
Narrative Poems

**SALIHAH MOORE KIRBY**

Light in the Darkness
Mysteries of Time
Prophets & Saints

**AMADINE KIRBY, AGE 9**

Singing & Dancing

**LATEEFA SPIKER**

Pilgrimage
Signs of Allah (original lino print)
Prayer (original lino print)

**SORAYA SYED**

On Death & Dying (original calligraphy, "Al-Quddus," from the cover of Holy Door in the Ground, Ecstatic Exchange, 2018)

*No images may be copied or reproduced in any form without permission from the artist or their estate.*